GLORIA"S GUY
A PLAY BY JOAN BURROWS

PLAYWRIGHTS CANADA PRESS
TORONTO

LIBRARY AND ARCHIVES CANADA CATALOGUING IN PUBLICATION
Burrows, Joan, author
       Gloria's Guy / Joan Burrows.

A play.
Issued in print and electronic formats.
ISBN 978-1-77091-888-7 (softcover).--ISBN 978-1-77091-889-4 (PDF).--
ISBN 978-1-77091-890-0 (EPUB).--ISBN 978-1-77091-891-7 (Kindle)

I. Title.

PS8553.U6946G46 2018   C812'.6   C2018-900471-1
                                               C2018-900472-X

Playwrights Canada Press acknowledges that we operate on land which, for thousands of years, has been the traditional territories of the Mississaugas of the New Credit, the Huron-Wendat, the Anishinaabe, Métis, and the Haudenosaunee peoples. Today, this meeting place is still home to many Indigenous people from across Turtle Island and we are grateful to have the opportunity to work and play here.

We acknowledge the financial support of the Canada Council for the Arts—which last year invested $153 million to bring the arts to Canadians throughout the country—the Ontario Arts Council (OAC), the Ontario Media Development Corporation, and the Government of Canada for our publishing activities.

 Canada Council   Conseil des arts
for the Arts   du Canada

 ONTARIO ARTS COUNCIL
CONSEIL DES ARTS DE L'ONTARIO
an Ontario government agency
un organisme du gouvernement de l'Ontario

 Canada

 Ontario
Ontario Media Development
Corporation

To the Alumnae Theatre, celebrating its one hundredth anniversary of developing women in theatre, and especially to the New Play Development group of women writers for their continued support and wise counsel.

Gloria's Guy was first produced by the Alumnae Theatre, Toronto, as part of their first FireWorks Festival from November 13 to December 1, 2013, with the following company:

Peggy: Jennifer Monteith
Guy: Robert Meynell
Jessie: Liz Best
Gloria: Anna Douglas
Eva: Erin Jones
Leslie: Sangeeta Wylie

Producer: Dahlia Katz
Director: Anne Harper
Stage Manager: Edgar Chua
Set and Lighting Design: Ed Rosing
Sound Design: Gabrielle D'Angelo
Costume Design: Bec Brownstone
Properties: Tess Hendaoui and Tara Gostling

CHARACTERS

Peggy
Guy
Jessie
Gloria
Eva
Leslie

ACT 1
SCENE 1

The setting is the upper floor of a furnished resort boathouse. A large picture window in the upstage wall looks out to the lake, and distant trees are showing the early colours of autumn. Beside this window is an entrance consisting of a locked door and a screen door. The main room has a couch, a smaller chair, and a coffee table on an area rug. There is a counter with basic kitchenware and a small refrigerator. Downstage right is the door to the bathroom and above this is another door to a bedroom. A door stage left leads to a second bedroom. The room is neat and ready for its weekend guests. Margaret "PEGGY" Anne McConnell, carrying a large garment bag and grocery bags, walks in front of the picture window and then unlocks the door. She enters.

PEGGY   Oh my God! The boathouse suite! Looks exactly the same.

           Offstage voices are heard.

JESSIE   How much farther?

She turns her attention to the voices stage right.

PEGGY   Are you okay, Ma? Just a few more steps up. Do you need any help?

JESSIE   I'm fine. Guy's right behind me. You're still there, right, Guy?

GUY   Don't worry, Mrs. McConnell. I've got your rear.

JESSIE   Don't be cheeky, Guy.

GUY   Don't you be talking to me about cheeky.

> *PEGGY walks into the central room, putting the garment bag over the back of the couch and the grocery bags on the counter. She quickly does a check of the rooms beginning downstage left, crossing to the bathroom stage right and then disappearing into the bedroom door beside it. JESSIE and GUY appear in front of the window heading toward the door.*

That's it, Mrs. Mac! Door's on the right.

> *An older woman, maybe in her early seventies, dressed in pants and jacket enters winded and carrying a rather large garment bag, a sewing basket, and her purse.*

JESSIE   Oh my.

> *She crosses into the room and sits on the chair, still clutching the garment bag.*

> *GUY enters behind her. He is around forty, lean and casually dressed in jeans, T-shirt, denim jacket, and baseball cap. At*

the moment he is somewhat loaded down with weekend bags, a portable sewing machine, and yet another garment bag.

GUY   Sorry, Mrs. Mac. Pat opened the boathouse for the girls because it's what Peggy wanted. I don't think she realized you'd be coming with them. She could give you some rooms in the main building on the ground floor. Except for a few wedding guests, we're not very busy. Off-season and all.

JESSIE   I wasn't part of the original plan. But when some of the girls cancelled out, Margaret Anne asked if I wanted to come for the weekend rather than just for the wedding tomorrow. It seemed like a good idea considering there's still a few alterations to be made on the dresses. Especially your niece's.

PEGGY enters from the bedroom.

PEGGY   Are you all right, Ma? I forgot how many steps there were to get up here. Let me take the dresses.

She removes the garment bag from JESSIE's hands and hangs it up on a coat hook near the door. She does the same with the others while she continues the conversation.

It's just that we wanted the boathouse for old times' sake. A little nostalgia this weekend for Leslie's fortieth birthday.

GUY   I was just saying that Pat could find some rooms in the main building.

PEGGY   Oh, no. It'll be fine, won't it, Ma? We'll make sure you don't do the stairs too often. I'll get Kerry and the girls to come here to try on the dresses; more privacy from the groom.

JESSIE   It's fine, dear. But where will everyone sleep?

PEGGY   Well, you and I'll grab that room. It's got two single beds and next to the bathroom. In case you have to get up in the night.

JESSIE   Not in case, dear. When and how often is more like it.

PEGGY   Whoever arrives next can claim the other room and last in gets the couch. We'll set up the drinks and snacks and settle in for a good old-fashioned pyjama party. Just like back then. Care to join us, Guy? Can't promise the lingerie will be as interesting this time round though.

GUY   Thanks but Pat and Jimmy have me pretty busy with the rehearsal party tonight. It's my job to make sure the groom and his men don't go overboard and end up too hungover to watch the bride come down the aisle tomorrow afternoon. Besides, I don't wear PJs. Might be distracting—especially for you, Mrs. Mac.

JESSIE   Don't be so fresh, Guy. I may not teach you anymore but I still see your mother every Wednesday at the hospital guild. She wouldn't want me sharing that information with the other ladies, now would she?

GUY   *(laughing)* My mother's been shaking her head over me for a long time now.

JESSIE   You're telling me. When she used to start in on her Tales of Guy, it made the rest of us glad we had daughters! I need to freshen up, Margaret Anne. Then I'll help you with the dresses. Guy, be a dear and take the bags into that bedroom for us.

     JESSIE heads into the bathroom.

GUY   Good idea. Establish territory before the others arrive.

           PEGGY helps him with the bags.

PEGGY   Eva should be here soon. Leslie can't get up from the city
           until late. She's gonna be stuck in that traffic. You probably
           haven't seen her for years.

GUY   Uh . . . actually, I ran into her last spring, out in LA. We
           were at the same . . . party. My firm was representing some
           restaurateur opening a new place and she was there.

PEGGY   Oh? Funny she never mentioned it.

GUY   Since I've been home I see her picture constantly in the paper
           with some celebrity's arm around her. Allen's Bistro with
           a four-star rating. Who would've thought that our Leslie
           would become one of the major restaurateurs in the city?

PEGGY   She's done really well for herself. One of the success stories
           of our class.

GUY   The only success story.

PEGGY   What about you? Mr. LA Lawyer, no less!

GUY   Hello. Living in Woodsville now. Carrying luggage in my
           brother's resort. Those LA days are over.

PEGGY   But you're still a lawyer. You got further than most of us.

GUY   Further? I'm not so sure.

PEGGY   Look at it this way. You got the education. Leslie got the
          money. This weekend is sort of a surprise fortieth birthday
          party for her.

GUY   It'll be nice to see her again.

PEGGY   She's only here for tonight. Some film producer has booked
          her place for a wrap party tomorrow night so she has to get
          back to the city. I haven't seen her since Eva's wedding.

GUY   To the dentist?

PEGGY   Divorced that one. Seems teeth weren't the only things he
          was filling.

GUY   Oh.

PEGGY   She married Steve two years ago. He sells insurance. But
          knowing Eva the Diva, I'm sure we're in for more drama
          about husband number two. At least Leslie said she had
          some great news to share.

GUY   Another restaurant opening?

PEGGY   Probably! Maybe this one's in New York. Or maybe she's
          decided to open a place up here. She could buy you and your
          brother out, if you're interested.

GUY   I just put what little money I had into this place. But an
          Allen's North just a little farther up the shore sure could help
          us. People from the city could book to eat there but sleep
          here. We'd both win!

          He looks around and sees the bags are finished.

Okay, so you and Mrs. Mac have claimed the twin room. Eva can go there.

He points to the other bedroom.

I can't believe she agreed to have your mom tag along. Mrs. Mac scared the bejesus out of her in high school.

PEGGY   It'll be fine. Where's the extra linen for the couch?

GUY   Pat keeps it in this room.

He heads for the bedroom downstage left.

PEGGY   Eva'll probably let Gloria have that room so she can bunk out here and gab all night with Leslie.

GUY suddenly reappears in the doorway.

GUY   Gloria? Gloria Atherly?

PEGGY   Yeah. Didn't Pat tell you she was coming?

GUY   No.

PEGGY   Oh, well, when your sister asked me to make the wedding dresses, I bartered my time for a free weekend for all us girls at the resort. We've been trying to have a boathouse blast for years but something always gets in the way of our reunion. Even now two cancelled out and Leslie's only good for tonight. Gloria arranged for them all to play golf tomorrow morning but I guess she doesn't have a foursome now. She'll be so disappointed. Hey, maybe you could play with her?

GUY   Gloria Atherly is coming here for the weekend and you want me to play golf with her? Peggy, I haven't spoken to Gloria in years. Ever since that fiasco on grad night, we've managed to avoid each other.

PEGGY   Come on. Do you mean to say you haven't seen her in all that time?

GUY   Seen her? Yeah. If I was home for Christmas I'd see her and Charlie at church sitting with her dad. Or if we were here on the same weekend in the summer, I might catch sight of her coming out of a store. We'd do this weird head nod to each other.

            He demonstrates.

            Once, when I came out of Logan's Drugstore, I saw her on the other side of Main Street. It was just a few months after Charlie was killed. I did this really stupid wave—

            Again he demonstrates.

            But then this huge transport stopped at the light and when it lurched through the intersection she was gone. I don't even think she saw me. Does she know that I've moved back home?

PEGGY   I might've mentioned it. Don't worry, Guy. Gloria's not here this weekend to meet up with an old high-school sweetheart. She's coming up for some serious girl fun and to get in a little golf. Considering how you treated her on grad night back then, I seriously doubt she's gonna be chasing you around the hot tub. You can count on Eva to do that. Husband number two probably being on the way out and all.

GUY   Thanks for the warning. I'll stay clear of the boathouse for
           the rest of the weekend.

           JESSIE steps out of the bathroom.

JESSIE   Now why would you do that, Guy? Your mother tells me you
           haven't dated anyone since you've been home. Didn't even ask
           anyone to be your escort for your niece's wedding. What's
           wrong with you? Surely you're not going to stand there and
           tell us that Woodsville women just don't compare to those
           California blonds you were dating all those years. None of
           them seemed to last very long.

PEGGY   Ma!

GUY   You're right, Mrs. Mac. There's no comparison. That's why
           I had to leave the sun and surf and head back to the wilds
           of Woodsville. I needed to find a real woman in my life and
           where better than back here in my old hometown. After all,
           this town is teeming with them, right?

PEGGY   How about Marjorie Heckles, the librarian. She's available.
           She's sixty-three but she's still available. Or how about Rita
           down at Gary's Diner? I've seen you in there scarfing down
           her BLTs. What more could a man want? A woman who
           cooks.

GUY   How about a woman who cooks and has teeth!

JESSIE   Joke all you want, Guy Larkin, but you need a woman in
           your life. Just because your first marriage didn't last doesn't
           mean the second one won't. It's high time you climbed back
           into that saddle. Haven't you heard that song, "The Second
           Time Around"?

GUY   Could you hum me a few bars?

JESSIE   I'll give you more than a few bars. I'll give you verse and chorus if you find yourself a girl before Christmas.

GUY   Tell you what. I'll be on the lookout for someone as long as you're doing the same. After all, you've been widowed for some time now. Isn't it time you started to find someone for your saddle? You said it yourself—love can be wonderful the second . . .

JESSIE   My saddle's too old and worn out, thank you very much. And after forty-five years of marriage, I'm not looking for another rider. You, on the other hand, better find some filly fast before you forget how to ride.

PEGGY   Ma!

GUY   You mean it's not like a bike, Mrs. Mac? I thought once you learned you never forgot.

JESSIE   When you were a kid you fell off your bike all the time.

GUY   Trust me, I learned how to ride.

JESSIE   But have you learned how to hold on?

PEGGY   Ma, leave Guy alone. He's only been back a few months. If he's meant to settle down here, he will. Right, Guy?

GUY   Right, Peg. Hey, why don't I call Ted and he can be my wingman as I go cruisin' for babes. Of course, we can't cruise far seeing as there's only one street in town.

PEGGY   Be my guest. I'll have to warn you, though, Ted's usually asleep in front of the TV by ten, so don't count on it being a late night.

GUY   *(laughing)* See, Mrs. Mac, I'm trying but I'm blocked wherever I turn.

JESSIE   Laugh all you want, my boy. I just hope you're not laughing so hard that you don't see an opportunity when it presents itself to you. Opportunity only knocks once, you know.

GUY   Is that another song title?

PEGGY   Trust me, if it isn't, she'll turn it into one by the end of the weekend. Look, Ma, we need to finish the hem on Kerry's dress, so why don't you unpack your sewing stuff. I'll run over to see if Pat has an ironing board we can set up in here.

GUY   I'll get you one, Peg.

PEGGY   We'll need a steam iron, too.

GUY   No problem. I'll go down the back way to the resort. How about you, Mrs. Mac, need anything? Food? Drink? Man?

JESSIE   Just bring me a good heavy iron. I just thought of another use for it!

She mimes it as a weapon on GUY's *head.*

GUY   Mrs. Mac, how can I possibly find a woman if my head's cracked?

JESSIE   Same way you found that first one, I guess.

*GUY laughs and exits through the boathouse door, turning
stage left.*

PEGGY   Honestly, Ma, will you lay off? It can't be easy for him
coming back home and living here with Pat and Jimmy. We
all thought he had it made living out in California, hobnob-
bing with the rich and famous, making tons of money. But
obviously something wasn't right. Otherwise why would he
come back here?

JESSIE   His wife left him.

PEGGY   Yeah, well . . .

JESSIE   And she got custody of his child.

PEGGY   There's more to it. Does his mother ever say anything to you?

JESSIE   No. She used to regale us with all kinds of stories but she's
been pretty tight-lipped about Guy for the last few years.

PEGGY   He's come over to the house a few times to see Ted and,
I don't know, Guy's changed. He may seem all cheeky on
the outside but both Ted and I sense a real sadness in him.
Something happened. And so far, he hasn't shared anything
but I don't think teasing him about being single really helps,
so maybe . . .

JESSIE   Who's teasing? I'm serious. Maybe his sadness comes out of
loneliness. I just think he should be ready for whoever comes
into his life, that's all.

*GLORIA Atherly, slim, attractive, and casually but smartly
dressed appears in the picture window. She knocks on it,*

waves, and proceeds to the screen door. PEGGY *rushes to open it for her. They hug each other affectionately.*

PEGGY   Glorreeeaaa! Wow! Look at you. You look stunning. Doesn't she look stunning, Ma?

GLORIA   Me? You look wonderful. Hi, Mrs. McConnell.

         GLORIA *crosses to* JESSIE *and hugs her with affection as well.*

         I'm so glad you decided to come for our weekend. It's been too long.

JESSIE   Oh, Gloria. Since your dad moved to Florida you hardly ever come up to Woodsville anymore.

GLORIA   I know, I'm sorry. I come up a few times in the summer. Dad kept his cottage over at the lake. More for my brother and his family, but it's an occasional retreat for me, too. But when I'm there, I just don't feel like coming into town and battling the tourists, you know?

JESSIE   Well, that's understandable. Maybe you should just move back.

GLORIA   *(laughing)* You know, I spent my whole teenage existence wanting to get out of here as fast as I could, and now that I'm almost forty and living in the city with all the traffic and congestion and smog, I spend just as much time pining for Woodsville. An example of irony; something you taught me, Mrs. Mac.

JESSIE   Well, you can't always get what you want.

PEGGY God, another song title! You'll have a musical by the end of the weekend.

> PEGGY *pushes her mother into the bedroom.*

Listen, why don't you unpack before Gloria tours the boat-house and lays claim to our room.

(to GLORIA) Sorry but Ma and I have to deal with a last fitting of the dresses this afternoon.

GLORIA No problem. I'll just drop my stuff and take a run into town. Are we going to eat out or do you want me to pick up some dinner for us?

PEGGY Oh, would you mind? That way Ma doesn't have to do the stairs again. We can veg here all evening. Pat said the family will be busy with the rehearsal party tonight so we can use the pool and hot tub to our heart's content.

GLORIA The pool in October? Is it heated?

PEGGY I don't know. But the hot tub'll be lovely. Especially with a bottle of vino and lots of gossip to keep us warm.

GLORIA Gossip—must mean Eva's coming. I can't believe she was okay with your mom being part of the reunion.

> *Beat.*

PEGGY She doesn't know.

GLORIA What?

PEGGY   When the others cancelled, it just made sense for me to bring Ma out here. She's great at last-minute alterations. Besides, this way I don't have to drive all the way back into town tomorrow to pick her up. She wants to see the final products sashaying down the aisle. She's worked hard on these dresses and her eyesight and arthritis didn't make the job any easier for her.

GLORIA   How's she been doing since your dad died?

PEGGY   Better in some ways. At least now she has time to get involved with her life again. She threw herself into this wedding project. Hauled out the old Singer and we set up a production line on her dining-room table. I don't know what I would've done without her. So Eva can whine all she wants about Ma being here for our girls' weekend, but she's staying. Besides, I don't think she should be left alone too often.

GLORIA   What do you mean?

PEGGY   A few weeks ago I went over to her place to help Kerry with a fitting. Kerry asked for a glass of water and when I opened the freezer to get some ice, Ma's purse was sitting in there.

GLORIA   What was it doing in the freezer?

PEGGY   God knows. I wasn't gonna ask her in front of Kerry, and when Kerry left I didn't know how to broach the subject. It terrifies me that what happened to my dad is starting to happen to her. I don't think I can go through all of that again.

GLORIA   The freezer. That is weird. Have you noticed anything else?

PEGGY   Sometimes she calls me Jeannie or rather runs through all
             my sisters' names until she comes to me—"Abby, Jeannie,
             Margaret Anne—whatever your name is."

GLORIA   Oh, my dad did that for years.

PEGGY   And she mixes words up. Drives me crazy.

GLORIA   She seemed fine to me. But if I notice anything out of the
             ordinary, I'll let you know.

PEGGY   Thanks, Glory. I just hope Eva doesn't make the weekend
             miserable for her.

GLORIA   It'll be the opposite. Eva won't be able to be so outrageous.
             She was always a little terrified of your mother. If we have
             to hear all about what's wrong with husband number two,
             maybe we'll get a shortened version with your mom here.

             *JESSIE enters from the bedroom with the sewing basket and
             a wedding dress.*

JESSIE   I unpacked and hung up the dress I'm wearing tomorrow.
             I'll iron it out when we do the others. Has the ironing board
             arrived?

PEGGY   Guy's not back yet. I'll go see if I can find him and a couple
             of the bridesmaids. If we can get them out of the way, we
             can spend more time on Kerry's dress.

JESSIE   Hers is the one I'm most worried about considering what
             happened at the last fitting.

PEGGY   That's why I told Pat to send her here as soon as she arrives.

PEGGY exits.

GLORIA   Did Peggy say Guy was bringing an ironing board?

JESSIE   Yes, dear. Did you want to press out some things?

GLORIA   *(hurriedly)* No. No. I'm just going to put my stuff away and
then get out of your way for a while. I'll drive into town and
take a walk around. See what's new and different.

> *GLORIA quickly picks up her bag and heads into the bedroom
> stage left.*

JESSIE   Gloria, this is Woodsville. Nothing is new and different.

> *GUY walks in front of the window and enters the boathouse
> carrying an ironing board and an iron.*

GUY   Hey, Mrs. Mac, how's this for room service. I'll even set it
up for you. No charge. Where do you want it?

> *She indicates in front of GLORIA's door.*

JESSIE   Oh, over there, I guess. As long as it's out of the way.

> *GUY, with his back to the door, is busy putting up the ironing
> board, unaware of GLORIA who, unaware of GUY, backs out of
> her room, closing the door behind her. Suddenly they back into
> each other, turn, and stand inches from each other. There is an
> awkward moment and then an even more awkward head nod
> first from GUY and followed by GLORIA. JESSIE watches all of
> this with fascination. There is a long pause.*

Guy, you remember Gloria Atherly, don't you?

GUY   Huh? Oh, yeah. Sure. Hey, Glory. Gloria. Hi.

             He goes to shake hands but is holding the iron.

JESSIE   Gloria, you remember Guy, don't you? Weren't you all in the
             same class together?

GLORIA   Right. Yeah. Hello, Guy. Nice to see you again.

JESSIE   Again? Oh, you see each other regularly?

GUY &
GLORIA   No!

GUY   I mean. I've seen Glory . . . Gloria. On occasion. From a
             distance. When I've been home.

JESSIE   Oh, I see. Well, doesn't she look stunning, Guy? Margaret
             Anne and I were just saying how stunning she looked when
             she arrived.

GUY   Stunning. Yes.

GLORIA   Thanks. You look . . . good, too. You look very . . . relaxed.
             How've you been?

GUY   Uh, relaxed.

             Another pause.

JESSIE   *(prompting)* Guy's moved back to Woodsville, Gloria. He's
             part owner of the resort now with Jimmy and Pat.

GLORIA   I heard about that. From Peggy.

GUY   Yeah. A couple of months now . . . I came home at the beginning of the season . . . Thought I could help out around here for a bit.

Another pause.

JESSIE   *(prompting again)* And Gloria's still in the city. Still with the bank.

GUY   So you're still in the city? Still with the bank?

GLORIA   Yes.

Beat.

Yes.

GUY   That's good. Being with the bank. That's good.

GLORIA   Well, I was just heading out.

She starts to head toward the door.

JESSIE   Guy, why don't you go with Gloria and show her everything that's new in town.

GUY   Huh?

JESSIE   She hasn't seen the showcase in the library. Marjorie Heckles has that wonderful display on the gynecological chart of her family. It goes all the way back to the War of 1812.

GUY stares at JESSIE in disbelief.

GUY   They let her put that in the public library?

GLORIA   Do you mean genealogical chart, Mrs. McConnell?

JESSIE   Isn't that what I said? You should take that in.

JESSIE pushes them together.

Oh, and what about the new booths in Gary's Diner? I hear they're very comfortable. Maybe you two could go and have a coffee, try them out.

GLORIA   *(quickly)* I'm sure Guy's busy.

GUY   Uh, yeah. I, uh, have some work to do in the reception hall for the wedding tomorrow.

JESSIE   Do you need some help?

GUY   Huh?

JESSIE   Gloria could help you. There's nothing to see in town anyway.

GUY   Well, we're setting up tables and stuff. It's kind of dirty work. I wouldn't want you to . . .

GLORIA   *(quickly)* It's okay. I really need to run a few errands. Pick up dinner.

(to JESSIE) Tell Peggy I'll meet you here later. I'm sure Eva'll be here by then.

(turning) Goodbye, Guy. It was . . . nice to see you.

GUY   Bye, Glory. Gloria.

GLORIA exits. They watch as she passes the window and then JESSIE turns, glaring at GUY and giving his shoulder a swat.

Ow!

JESSIE You just let Gloria Atherly drive into town all on her own when you could've spent the rest of the afternoon with that lovely woman. You're not *relaxed*; you're pathetic.

GUY I didn't expect to see her so soon. I was hoping not to see her at all. Boy, that was awkward, wasn't it?

JESSIE Awkward? It was unbearable! What's wrong with you? Ten minutes ago you were as cheeky as all get out, maybe even a little charming, if you like that sort of thing. But in front of Gloria you turned into this . . . this . . . big head-nodding lug. Didn't you use to date Gloria years ago?

GUY I dated Gloria in our last year of high school, but we didn't end our friendship very well. Our prom date was a disaster and it was sort of my fault, I guess.

JESSIE Why? What'd you do?

GUY I didn't show up. I never went to get her.

JESSIE What?

GUY She had to go to the prom by herself. At around ten that night. Apparently she stayed fifteen minutes and then came out here to the boathouse. It was pretty humiliating for her.

JESSIE Where were you?

GUY   It's a long story. I tried to apologize to her. Some of the girls were staying here for that weekend and I came out to see her but she wouldn't speak to me. Two days later I left for a summer job at my uncle's logging camp in BC. Stayed there for university. Went south to California. We never connected. So anytime we've caught sight of each other over the years, it's always very . . . strained. Very . . . complicated. Especially after Charlie was killed. I wanted to write to her but I didn't know what to say.

JESSIE   How about "sorry"?

GUY   Which sorry? Sorry for the sudden and tragic loss of your husband? Sorry for being a jerk in high school? Sorry for being a coward all these years?

JESSIE   I like the last one. Start with that one.

GUY   It's more than that. There's things I need to say to Gloria but not now and not in front of somebody else.

JESSIE   I hate to tell you this but if I hadn't been standing here with the two of you just now, you would've been head-bobbin' the afternoon away. Gloria's only here for forty-eight hours, so you'd better find the time. She didn't wait for you on prom night. My sense is she won't wait for you now. And clean yourself up, for goodness' sakes.

    She knocks his hat off.

    Don't be trying to have a serious conversation when you look like Paul Bunyan.

GUY   Am I becoming your personal pity project, Mrs. Mac? What's it gonna take for you to lay off me?

JESSIE   Fine. I'll stop pestering you if you help me out with something before you head down to your tables and chairs. The hem of Kerry's wedding dress is uneven and I need to put it on someone. She's not here and I doubt Pat has a mannequin, so you'll have to do.

GUY   You want me to put on the wedding dress? Are you crazy?

She holds up the dress.

JESSIE   Oh for heaven's sakes, it'll only take a minute. You're about the same height when Kerry has her heels on and, let's be frank, we all know that her size keeps changing these days, so you should be about where she is now. Here, you need to step into it. Mind the pins. And don't put your grubby hands on it. Let me help you.

He struggles with the fitting.

GUY   Look, Mrs. Mac, I don't think this is such a good idea. I'm not model material.

JESSIE   Nonsense. Stop fidgeting and let me see if I can do up this zipper a bit so that the dress will fall more evenly. Hold on a sec.

She looks around for a small pillow that she places firmly in the stomach of the dress.

Good. That should be about where she is now, I would think. Now, turn around.

He spins around.

Slower. Slower. Let it fall naturally.

He turns again.

That's better. Now walk over there for me.

GUY   You're kidding, right?

JESSIE   Guy Larkin, stop being so stubborn. There's a spot in the back that's bothering me. I want to see what happens to it when you're moving. People are gonna be staring at the back of this dress for the entire ceremony.

He clomps to the other side of the room.

Oh for heaven's sakes, not like that. Kerry may be your niece and . . . a big girl, but she's got more grace than that. Now try again. Stop swinging those arms.

She rolls up a magazine and gives it to him.

Pretend you're carrying flowers.

He lumbers back, turns, and attempts to cross more gracefully.

GUY   How's this?

JESSIE   Better. Once more.

GUY   Mrs. Mac!

JESSIE   Guy!

He repeats the walk.

There, I see the problem. Stay still a minute until I readjust a few pins.

She kneels down behind him to fix the dress.

So . . . why don't you drop by this evening after the rehearsal party? The others'll be here. They'd love to see you. And you'd be dressed better, right?

GUY Look, Mrs. Mac, I know what you're trying to do and you can stop, okay?

JESSIE What do you mean?

GUY Trying to line me up with Gloria Atherly. It's not gonna work. For a lot of reasons.

JESSIE Such as?

GUY We don't have anything in common any more.

JESSIE How do you know?

GUY She lives in the city. I live here.

JESSIE You used to live in a city. She used to live here. I'd say you share geographical knowledge. Next excuse.

GUY These aren't excuses. Just facts.

JESSIE Well, how about the fact that you're both single? How about the fact that you've both had your hearts broken? In different ways, of course, but you both know what it's like to lose someone. How about that you used to be best friends? You liked each other. In fact, I remember one night, many years ago, Margaret Anne was prattling on about you and something that had happened in school that day. She kept repeating the phrase "glorious guy," *"glorious guy."* It took me a few minutes to realize she wasn't complimenting you. She was explaining who you were. You had become *Gloria's guy*. At eighteen, that was a pretty good person to be.

GUY   Yeah, well at eighteen I made some pretty stupid choices.

JESSIE   Oh, get over it, for heaven's sakes. That was high school. This is middle age. I'm sure Gloria has long forgotten and forgiven.

GUY   Mrs. Mac, I don't think any girl gets over being dumped at her prom. And I'm not middle-aged.

JESSIE   Well, how're you gonna know if you don't find out?

            Standing up and turning him around to face her.

            Now, I expect you to show up here tonight. In better clothes. Lose the hat. And spend some time with her. Take her on a tour of the place.

            (suddenly) I know. Why not ask if she wants to go in the hot tub?

GUY   The hot tub? You are certifiable, Mrs. Mac, you know that? Gloria Atherly is not gonna climb into a hot tub with me after almost twenty years of us hardly speaking to each other.

JESSIE   You never know. I can help by keeping the others busy. But you have to want to be here. Now walk back and forth once more and you're done.

            GUY crosses back and forth. GLORIA suddenly appears in the window and watches him execute a slow but graceful turn. GUY catches sight of her and lets out a scream. GLORIA hastily moves to the front door. Mortified, GUY *struggles to get out of the dress as* GLORIA *enters the room.*

GLORIA   I don't mean to interrupt, but I got all the way down to the car and realized I'd forgotten my keys. I'll just be a second.

She crosses into her room.

JESSIE   Be careful, Guy! One of these side seams is only basted. Don't rip the dress, for heaven's sakes.

GUY   At this moment, I really hate you, Mrs. Mac. I really do.

JESSIE   Don't worry. She hardly noticed. At least you're a little more dressed up.

GUY   Get me out of this!

He fumbles to get out of the dress and falls into GLORIA *just as she is entering from the bedroom with her purse and keys. They fall to the floor together. There is a horrible awkward moment where they look at each other.* GUY *nods his head.* GLORIA *returns the nod.*

Are you all right? I'm sorry.

He stands up, holding the dress around his knees, and sticks his hand out to help her but she is too busy crawling around looking for her keys. When he realizes what she is doing, he drops to the floor to help as she stands up.

GLORIA   Here they are.

She rises, looks down at him, and holds out her hand.

Can I help you up? I wouldn't want you to rip your dress.

GUY finally takes the dress off.

GUY   It's not my dress! It's Kerry's! And I'm done here! All right, Mrs. Mac? Done! Now if you'll excuse me, I'm going down to the reception hall to carry tables and chairs. Which are really heavy!

He heads to the door.

JESSIE   Yes, dear. That's a very manly thing to do now, isn't it? But let me know when you're finished.

GUY   Why?

JESSIE   The maid of honour's dress needs some buttons down the back.

GUY storms out. JESSIE and GLORIA watch him cross in front of the window.

JESSIE motions to GLORIA.

Not yet. Give it a second.

They wait and he returns to see if they're laughing. JESSIE gives a little wave. When he backs away the two women turn and laugh.

Poor Guy. He may never speak to me again.

GLORIA   Maybe that's a good thing. What was he doing?

JESSIE   Helping me out. Such a sweet man.

GLORIA   *(sarcastically)* Sure.

JESSIE   No, really. He's been so helpful this weekend. He's not just excited about his niece's wedding. He seemed really glad to hear about everyone who was coming. Especially you.

GLORIA   Me?

JESSIE   Oh, yes. Asked all kinds of questions about you. When would you be arriving? What you'd be doing.

GLORIA   Guy? Asking questions about me? I find that a little hard to believe, Mrs. McConnell. Guy has hardly acknowledged my existence these last twenty some years. I doubt he'd care about me being here this weekend. He can hardly stand to be in the same room with me.

JESSIE   Think what you like, Gloria, but that is an interested man if I ever saw one. Now, I'm gonna take this sewing machine into the bedroom as there's a desk in there right under the window with lots of light.

GLORIA   Here, I'll carry it for you.

JESSIE   Thanks.

         JESSIE looks over the wedding dress.

    I hope he didn't break the stitches. By the way, Gloria, did you bring a bathing suit?

GLORIA   Yes.

JESSIE   Good.

They exit stage right into the bedroom just as PEGGY *crosses in front of the window with* EVA.

PEGGY   *(entering)* Her car's still down front. She's probably still here.

PEGGY crosses to GLORIA'*s room with* EVA, *a middle-aged woman who dresses as if she's still in high school and has outrageously coloured hair. She carries her purse, her bag, and a cooler.*

Gloria! Look who's here.

EVA   Gosh, Peg, girl! You were right. This place looks exactly the same. In fact, I think that's the same blanket I threw up on twenty years ago! I'm calling dibs on that one. Just in case.

She walks over to the counter and begins unloading her cooler—wine bottles, coolers, a bottle of tequila, lemons, and a six pack of beer.

Hey, any glasses?

PEGGY   I brought some in a bag . . . *(looking around)* which I must've put in that room.

EVA starts toward the bedroom stage right.

No! I'll get them.

At that moment GLORIA *comes out of the bedroom.*

GLORIA   Eva the Diva!

GLORIA crosses to embrace EVA.

My God! Look at you. You look . . . exactly the same.

EVA   I'm not sure if that's a compliment or not! My kids complain that I never change my look. But why spoil a good thing, right? But you—you look awesome.

> *PEGGY comes out from the bedroom with the glasses and closes the door behind her.*

So are you two grabbing that room?

GLORIA   Actually, I put my stuff in that room. I was just in there helping . . .

PEGGY   *(suddenly and loudly)* I think we all look pretty damn good, given what we've been through.

> *They look oddly at her. PEGGY hands the glasses to EVA, who heads to the counter to open a bottle of wine.*

EVA   I'll drink to that. You have no idea how much I was looking forward to this weekend. We're gonna have a blast! No kids. No husband! Just the six of us sittin' round the hot tub, talkin' old times, catchin' up on gossip, drinkin' our brains out. Hey, maybe we can even do each other's hair tonight. I brought a couple of rinses with me. I was thinking of going blue. That would scare the hell out of the kids. And Steve.

> *EVA lifts her glass in a toast.*

Who wants to do it with me?

> *They grimace.*

No takers, eh? I bet Sheila will! Is that her in the other room?

She starts to cross.

PEGGY   *(quickly)* Actually, Sheila had to cancel. Sick child.

EVA   *(disappointed)* Ah, hell! Sheila's not coming? That sucks.

GLORIA   Francie sent regrets as well. Something about a shift change at the hospital.

EVA   Crap! The Stick's still comin' though, isn't she? I mean, it's her birthday! I'm countin' on her for tons of gossip this weekend. Everyone who's anyone eats at her restaurant these days!

PEGGY   Oh, yeah. Leslie's heading up later tonight.

EVA   Great. So did you call any replacements? Or is it just the four of us?

The sound of a sewing machine is heard from the bedroom. EVA looks at the door of the room, then at PEGGY.

Please don't tell me Allison Beasley's in there. Please not her.

PEGGY   No! I'd never call her without clearing it with all of you.

EVA   Thank Christ! Jeez, who the hell is the mystery guest?

EVA crosses quickly into the doorway of the bedroom before PEGGY can stop her. The sewing machine stops.

Oh. Hello, Mrs. McConnell.

JESSIE   Hello, Eva.

Slowly backing out from the bedroom, EVA turns and hisses to PEGGY.

EVA   You brought your mother to our pyjama party?

PEGGY smiles weakly and downs her drink. Lights out.

SCENE 2

The lights come up on the boathouse suite later that evening. The curtains on the upstage window are closed. There is evidence the pyjama party has started. The ironing board is gone and the bar has been used. There are several magazines strewn over the couch. A putter leans up against the wall outside GLORIA's bedroom. JESSIE, now in a long housecoat, is sitting on the chair searching through her purse for a nail file. Just as she is attending to her broken nail, there is a loud knock on the door. Startled, she sits up, reaches for her purse, and attempts to hide it in various places until she spies the refrigerator and puts it inside.

JESSIE   Coming . . . Just a moment . . . Be right there.

She opens the door to find GUY standing in the threshold looking sharp dressed in a sports jacket and dress pants. He carries a pie plate covered in foil and a bag of plastic plates and forks.

Oh, it's you. You scared the devil out of me.

GUY Sorry, Mrs. Mac.

    GUY looks around.

    Uh, where is everybody?

JESSIE They're down in the hot tub.

GUY Oh.

JESSIE Don't worry, they'll be back. Well, don't you look much improved. I'm glad to see you took my advice.

GUY I'm just coming from the rehearsal dinner. Pat had a ton of extra food left over so she sent up this pie for your soiree. There's plates and forks in the bag. Where should I put it?

JESSIE Oh, how nice! What kind is it?

GUY I'm not sure. There were three or four left over. I just grabbed one.

JESSIE Put it on the coffee table. We just finished dinner, but I'm sure we'll make a dent in this when the girls get back. So have you come with a game plan?

GUY What?

JESSIE A game plan? A master idea? How you're gonna get your talk in with Gloria?

GUY I've been thinking about it, Mrs. Mac, and I really don't think it's gonna happen. Not this weekend, anyway. Maybe another time.

JESSIE   If not this weekend, when? You may live here now, but Gloria doesn't. She rarely comes home anymore. Her dad moved to Florida. Charlie's parents are gone. Occasionally she visits the family cottage in summer, but that's clear on the other side of Whistle Lake. When do you expect to see her again? On the off chance she's walking down Main Street two years from now? She has no reason to be in Woodsville. But I bet she'd visit if you gave her a reason.

GUY   What am I supposed to say? Gee, Glory, it was great seeing you. Why don't you drive all the way back up here again next weekend so we can nod heads at each other? That's always so much fun!

JESSIE   Find something to do with her.

          She looks around, spying GLORIA's *new putter.*

          Here. Gloria just bought this when she and Eva went into town this afternoon. She's dying to use it. She loves to golf. You golf, don't you?

GUY   No.

JESSIE   What do you mean, no? What lawyer doesn't golf? And a Californian one at that?

GUY   Okay, I've golfed, but I'm not that great at it. It's a very expensive sport and it takes a lot of time. I worked in a law firm, not on a golf course.

JESSIE   I thought all you guys took your clients out to those fancy golf clubs just so you could close a few deals.

GUY   Look, Mrs. Mac, I worked in probate. I helped people write their wills. The last place they wanted to be when deciding who gets what was on a golf course. Nothing like a reminder that while the rest of the world would be enjoying sunshine and fresh air, they're gonna be six feet under. Besides, Gloria was always a way better athlete than I was anyway.

JESSIE   Perfect! That's your in.

GUY   Huh?

JESSIE   Ask her out to golf tomorrow morning. Show her how pathetic you are. She'll immediately feel sorry for you and insist on coming back next weekend to give you some lessons.

GUY   *(grimacing)* I don't know.

          He takes the putter and practises a few putts.

JESSIE   The girls'll be back soon. Can you come up with something better?

GUY   Look, she won't want to golf with me.

JESSIE   Nonsense. I heard her lament to Margaret Anne that she went out and bought this new putter but she won't even get a chance to use it. The others cancelled and, trust me, Gloria will not be keen to spend the morning alone with Eva, even if it is on a golf course. There's only so much any of us can listen to about husband number two. So all we have to do is get Eva out of the way and then you can spend the morning out on the links with Gloria Atherly.

GUY   How do you propose to stop Eva from coming with us?

JESSIE   Switch Gloria's tee-off time from ten to eight. Say there was a mix-up of some kind. There's no way Eva will be out of bed and functioning at eight a.m. I'll make sure Gloria is downstairs and waiting for you bright and early.

She pushes him toward the door and opens it.

Now go. The girls'll be back any minute. Come back and apologize for the time change and offer to go with her. She'll hardly refuse in front of the others. Besides, she'll take head-nodding with you over Eva's complaints any time.

Giggling bubbles up from outside.

Oh, no. They're back. You need to make an entrance. Hide.

GUY heads for the bathroom, putter in hand.

Not in there. That's the first place they'll go. Quick! In here.

She points to her bedroom and pushes him inside.

I'll get you out as soon as the coast is clear.

She pushes him in, turns, and sees the pie. She retrieves the pie, scurries back, hands it to GUY, and closes the bedroom door just as the girls are opening the front door. They have been in the hot tub and are slightly giddy. EVA has a bath towel wrapped around her and carries her wet bathing suit, a plastic glass, and an empty wine bottle. The others wear sweatsuits or jogging suits and carry towels and empty plastic glasses.

PEGGY   *(laughing)* God, Eva, I can't believe you did that. And with such ease. Did you see the look on their faces?

GLORIA   See it? I thought I was gonna have to lift the groom's jaw up from the side of the hot tub so she could get out. You're still outrageous, Eva, even at this age.

EVA   What? You've never wriggled out of a bathing suit before?

GLORIA   Not in front of four twenty-year-old males.

PEGGY   Well, not lately, anyway!

          JESSIE enters but stands guarding her door.

JESSIE   What have you girls been up to?

          The women turn suddenly to see her.

PEGGY   Oh, Ma, you should've come with us. There we were bubbling away in the hot tub when suddenly Kerry's fiancé and his groomsmen arrived. I guess the rehearsal dinner was too dull for them. Well, it's really dark and hard to make out faces so Eva says in a Southern drawl . . .

          She looks at EVA to continue.

EVA   Sorry, gentlemen, we weren't expectin' company tonight, so we three ladies are in here . . . naked. We could probably squeeze you in, but if we're in the buff, then you'll have to be too.

PEGGY   So these four guys look at each other really sheepishly and then one of them, I think it's the best man, says, "What the hell!" He throws down his towel, strips out of his suit, and climbs in. Just like that! The cheek of the kid. Not to be outdone, the others followed, except Kerry's fiancé was a little hesitant.

GLORIA   It didn't help that you called him by name.

PEGGY   "Why hello there, Bobby Seyfert; how's every little thing with you?"

GLORIA   And he's squinting in the dark saying, "Is that you, Mrs. Wayburn? Jeez!"

PEGGY   Anyways, he takes enough kidding from the others and suddenly yanks off his suit and in he comes. So there's this awkward moment of settling in and Bobby feels the need to introduce everyone. There's Glory and me trying to stay scrunched below the water, nodding and shaking hands when suddenly Eva says . . .

EVA   *(in her Southern drawl)* "Ladies, I think I've had quite enough. We don't want to turn into prunes in front of these charmin' young men, now do we?"

PEGGY   At which point, Gloria and I stand up . . .

GLORIA   Fully swimsuited . . .

PEGGY   And climb out of the tub. Well, you should've heard the shouts coming from those guys. The whining! Then, in this little lull, Eva stands up buck naked and says à la Blanche DuBois:

EVA   "I have always relied on the kindness of strangers. Which one of you fine young gentlemen is gonna help me climb out of this little ol' hot tub?"

GLORIA   They were so stunned. Didn't know what to do!

PEGGY   Deer in the headlights! One of them finally stood up to help her. Which one was it?

EVA   The first one. And trust me, he's not called the best man for nothing!

The women roar with laughter.

PEGGY   And then she added fuel to the fire by slapping her hands together—

EVA demonstrates.

—implying that he was putting his hands where he shouldn't. Scared the hell out of him! We could still hear Bobby berating him even as we climbed the stairs just now.

They continue to laugh.

What I don't understand is how you got out of your suit so fast?

EVA   Easy. While you all were shakin' hands, I just shimmied out of it. Comes from experience, I guess.

They look at her.

Haven't you ever changed your clothes in the car?

PEGGY   Sure.

EVA   While driving? It's a fine art, trust me.

JESSIE   I'm glad I wasn't there. God knows what damage would've been done to those boys if I had participated.

The girls look at her and then laugh.

EVA   Who wants another drink?

GLORIA   I want to change out of this wet suit first.

             She goes into her room.

PEGGY   Me too, and I'm gonna switch to some soda water for a while.
             Sitting in the hot tub has made me really thirsty.

             *They start to cross to their rooms when JESSIE suddenly
             calls out.*

JESSIE   Is there any more tea, Margaret Anne?

PEGGY   I don't know. I made you a pot before we went downstairs.
             Did you drink the whole thing?

JESSIE   I don't remember.

             PEGGY crosses to the counter.

PEGGY   The pot's still pretty heavy. I'll pour you some more. Where's
             your mug?

JESSIE   Right here, dear.

             *JESSIE brings her mug to PEGGY, and as soon as the tea is
             poured she quickly guides PEGGY to the bathroom.*

             You should go into the bathroom and take off that wet bath-
             ing suit. Rinse it out right now. Nothing's worse than that
             chloroform smell.

PEGGY looks at her mother.

PEGGY   Chlorine, Ma.

JESSIE   That too.

       She pushes her daughter inside.

I'll get your pyjamas for you.

       JESSIE turns and sees EVA at the bar.

Eva . . . you haven't seen the bridesmaids' dresses yet, have you? Oh, they're lovely. I'll just get one to show you.

       She pushes the door of her bedroom open and we hear a bump.

Oops! Forgot I put that suitcase there.

       She hurries inside and returns immediately with pyjamas, which she throws into the bathroom, and a bridesmaid's dress.

PEGGY   Hey!

JESSIE   Sorry, dear.

       She hurries the bridesmaid's dress over to EVA.

Isn't it just a lovely colour? I don't think Gloria has seen this either. Here.

       JESSIE grabs EVA and takes her over to GLORIA's room. She knocks.

Just us, Gloria.

She opens the bedroom door.

I was just showing a bridesmaid's dress to Eva and thought you should see it too. Why don't the two of you look at it in here?

She thrusts EVA and the dress inside, closing the door. She then turns her attention to her bedroom door and rushes over to open it.

Quick, get outside.

GUY comes out with a rather flattened pie that JESSIE motions for him to get rid of. He puts it back in the bedroom and then starts toward the front door, which JESSIE has opened. Just as he's about to go out, PEGGY calls from the bathroom.

PEGGY   You were right, Ma.

JESSIE pushes GUY, hiding him behind the opened door so he is up against the wall of the cabin. She stands in front of it to hide him.

PEGGY enters shaking out her wet bathing suit.

My suit reeked of chlorine. I should've brought a little bag of detergent with me.

PEGGY stops, seeing her mother in the opened door.

What're you doing?

JESSIE   Just looking at the lake. It's really lovely this time of year.

PEGGY   Ma, it's pitch black out there. If it wasn't for the porch light, you couldn't see two feet in front of you.

JESSIE   Not looking, really. Just listening to the water . . . the waves sound so . . . peaceful.

PEGGY   Ma, it's a small lake, not an ocean. Are you all right?

JESSIE   Just having a hot flash, dear.

PEGGY   You still get those?

JESSIE   When they're convenient.

PEGGY   Huh?

JESSIE   Occasional. I meant to say . . . occasionally.

> *EVA, still in her towel, and* GLORIA, *now in lounging pyjamas, enter from the other bedroom with the dress.*

GLORIA   It's very pretty, Mrs. McConnell. I love how you did the buttons.

PEGGY   What are you doing with that?

GLORIA   Your mom gave it to us.

PEGGY   When?

GLORIA   Just now.

> PEGGY *turns to her mother.*

PEGGY   Why?

JESSIE   They hadn't seen it.

PEGGY   Oh.

> *Pause*

> Okay. I'll put it back in the bedroom.

>> *She takes it from GLORIA and goes into her room. There is an awkward pause as the girls look at JESSIE in the open doorway. She smiles at them and fans herself. EVA heads to the counter for her drink while GLORIA sits on the couch. PEGGY comes out still carrying the dress but now has the squashed pie in her other hand.*

> Ma, what's this?

>> *Beat.*

JESSIE   It's a pie, dear.

PEGGY   What was it doing on the bedroom floor?

JESSIE   Was that where it was? I was wondering what I had done with it.

PEGGY   You brought a pie?

JESSIE   Yes.

>> *PEGGY looks at it.*

PEGGY   But it's . . . squashed.

>> *She lifts the lid.*

What kind is it?

JESSIE   What does it look like?

PEGGY   You don't know?

JESSIE   I baked it a while ago. I forgot what kind I made.

PEGGY   It looks like lemon meringue. But why is it so flat?

JESSIE   Well . . . I packed it . . . in my suitcase.

PEGGY   You packed a pie in your suitcase?

>*PEGGY looks at GLORIA, who has become interested in their exchange, with a "do you see what I mean?" look.*

JESSIE   I'm sure it still tastes okay. There's plates and forks on the table.

>*They all look over to see the plastic bag.*

>*PEGGY crosses to the table.*

PEGGY   You packed plates and forks, too?

>*GLORIA takes the pie from PEGGY.*

GLORIA   *(in a low voice)* That's a good sign, isn't it? She remembered to bring everything.

>*PEGGY returns to her room with the dress.*

I'd love a piece, Mrs. McConnell, but I'm still full from dinner. How be we leave it here and get into it later?

PEGGY comes back out with GLORIA's putter in her hand.

PEGGY   Why is Gloria's putter in our room?

They all look at the putter, then at JESSIE.

JESSIE   Uh . . . I was practising . . . while you were out.

PEGGY   Practising?

JESSIE   Yes.

PEGGY   You were putting? In the bedroom?

JESSIE   Yes.

GLORIA   I didn't know you golfed, Mrs. McConnell.

PEGGY   She doesn't.

JESSIE   That's why I was practising. To see if I was any good at it . . . *(laughing)* I'm not.

GLORIA   It's difficult to get the ball into the cup, isn't it?

JESSIE   Ball?

PEGGY   You didn't use a golf ball?

JESSIE   No . . . I imagined one.

Beat.

EVA   Then how do you know you missed?

JESSIE   *(glaring at EVA)* I imagined I missed.

PEGGY   Ma, are you all right?

JESSIE   I'm fine.

PEGGY   It's getting a little chilly in here. Do you think you could close the door now?

JESSIE   Soon, dear.

JESSIE fans herself.

You know, the girls haven't seen the bride's dress. Why don't you take them into the bedroom and show it to them? Margaret Anne has done the most wonderful job on it.

GLORIA   I saw it, Peg. It's lovely.

PEGGY   When did you see it?

GLORIA   This aft. Guy Larkin was modelling it for your mom.

PEGGY turns to her mother.

PEGGY   You had Guy Larkin wearing Kerry's wedding dress?

JESSIE   I was just checking the hem.

EVA   Guy Larkin? Wow! There's a name from the past. I heard he's moved back. What's he look like? Betcha he hasn't aged much living that California lifestyle.

PEGGY   He looks good.

JESSIE *(a little too loudly)* I think he looks very handsome, don't you, Gloria?

    The door bumps her.

    GLORIA *has picked up a magazine and started to flip through it.*

GLORIA Hard to tell. I don't think white's his colour.

EVA I heard he's single again. That's interesting.

PEGGY Yeah. But don't start getting any ideas, Eva.

EVA What do you mean?

PEGGY You're married and he's not looking for anyone.

JESSIE Or, rather, he's not looking for anyone who's married. I wouldn't say he's not looking. If there was an attractive, intelligent, interesting, single woman in the room—

    The door bumps her again.

I'm sure Guy would be looking.

EVA I'd love to see him again.

JESSIE I thought there was a picture of him in that magazine Gloria has. It was some TV person, but when I first saw the picture, I thought to myself, what is Guy Larkin doing in an old *People* magazine?

    EVA *moves onto the sofa with* PEGGY, *taking hold of the magazine with her.*

EVA   Where?

JESSIE   Somewhere in the middle, I think.

> *The three girls are now concentrated on flipping through the magazine as JESSIE swings open the door and pushes GUY outside.*

EVA   Are we on the right page?

PEGGY   Keep flipping.

EVA   I don't see anyone who looks like Guy.

PEGGY   Are you sure you weren't imagining this, too?

JESSIE   Why speak of the devil! Look who's here.

> *The girls turn to see GUY standing in the screened doorway.*

Don't you look handsome, all dressed up. What brings you to the boathouse?

> *JESSIE takes his arm and brings him into the room, closing the door behind them.*

GUY   Uh . . . Pat sent me up with extra dessert.

> *He suddenly realizes he isn't carrying anything.*

JESSIE   And you thought you should check to see if we wanted any. How nice. But we have a pie already.

> *EVA rushes over to hug GUY, who is aware that she is still only wrapped in a towel.*

EVA   Guy! What a surprise. How are you? You haven't changed
          a bit.

GUY   Gosh, there, Eva. Neither have you.

          *He's not quite sure where to put his hands and finally disen-
          tangles himself from EVA.*

          So how's the . . . uh . . . *(looking at her towel)* pyjama party
          going? Can I get anything for you?

          *EVA leads him over and into the chair and then sits on
          the arm.*

EVA   You can get yourself comfortable and talk to us. It's so great
          to see you. After all these years. How about a drink?

GUY   No. Nothing, thanks.

EVA   Oh, come on, Guy. You can't just sit here and not have a
          drink for old times' sakes. Peggy, grab a beer from the fridge
          for Guy.

GUY   No, really. No beer.

EVA   How about some tequila, then. I even brought some limes.

GUY   No, thanks.

EVA   Guy!

GUY   A soda then. A soda would be fine.

          PEGGY moves to the fridge to find one.

EVA   A soda? Oh, I get it. You're saving yourself for the big wed-
             ding tomorrow.

             PEGGY opens the fridge to find her mother's purse.

PEGGY   Ma, isn't this yours?

JESSIE   Why, yes it is.

PEGGY   What's it doing in the fridge?

JESSIE   *(laughing)* I put it there when . . .

             JESSIE suddenly looks to GUY.

             . . . I thought it would be . . . I really don't know.

             PEGGY gives a knowing look to GLORIA.

             But thank you for finding it for me, Margaret Anne.

             *PEGGY opens a soda and gives it to GUY while still looking
             at her mother.*

PEGGY   Here you go, Guy.

             He gets out of the chair but EVA follows him.

             EVA clinks her wine glass against GUY's can.

EVA   Cheers!

JESSIE   Did you find that picture of Guy, Gloria?

JESSIE crosses to GUY and pushes him onto the sofa beside GLORIA.

I came across a picture in this old *People* magazine that I could have sworn was you. Look through it with Gloria to see if you can find it.

GLORIA and GUY look uncomfortably at each other and nod.

GUY   Trust me, Mrs. Mac, I'm not in any *People* magazine.

EVA   But, Guy, all those years in LA. You can't tell me you haven't partied with the rich and famous.

GUY   Rich and infamous, maybe. But not the people in here.

He points to the magazine.

If you want gossip about the famous, you're gonna have to talk to Leslie. Where is she? I thought she was coming to your reunion.

PEGGY   She should be here. Maybe the Friday-night traffic was worse than she expected.

EVA   I can't wait to see her. The last time I saw her, her hair was pink!

GUY   It was more purple when I saw her.

GLORIA   When did you see her?

GUY   Uh, about eight months ago. She was in LA and we sort of bumped into each other at a . . . restaurant. We had our own little reunion.

GLORIA   Funny, she never mentioned that.

EVA   And I hear you're home now. Why would you ever leave sunny Los Angeles? What could possibly bring you home?

           The others all look at GUY *and there is an awkward silence. And then a small knock at the door and a woman's voice calling out "Peggy?"*

PEGGY   *(in a loud whisper)* It's Leslie. Everybody hide and then yell "surprise!" when I open the door.

           (to the door) Coming.

           GLORIA *and* GUY *hide in front of the sofa and then realize how uncomfortably close they are to each other.* GLORIA *gets up and moves to her bedroom doorway while* EVA *pushes* GUY *over and crawls into the sofa space with him.* JESSIE, *who has crossed to her bedroom door, comes down and climbs over the sofa to be in the middle of* GUY *and* EVA. GUY *uses this opportunity to crawl away from the sofa and go into the bathroom doorway.* PEGGY *crosses to the boathouse door.*

           (whispering) On the count of three . . . One . . . two . . . three—

           She opens the door. Immediately a very large and pregnant LESLIE *enters the room carrying an overnight bag.*

LESLIE   *(as others jump up)* Surprise!

           They all stare at her in shock. They gasp and then turn to look at GUY.

           Blackout.

ACT 2
SCENE 1

Everyone is in the same positions they were in when PEGGY *opened the door. Everyone is staring at* GUY. *There is total silence.*

LESLIE   *(hesitant)* Surprise?

        They slowly look back at LESLIE.

What? I know it's a shock but . . .

        They all look back at GUY.

PEGGY   Guy?

        JESSIE *gets up from the sofa, crosses to* GUY, *and punches him in the arm.*

GUY   Ow!

LESLIE   Guy?

LESLIE suddenly sees him.

Oh, Guy. I was hoping I'd run into you again. I've so much to tell you.

EVA   No kidding!

JESSIE hits him again.

JESSIE   How could you?

GUY   Ow! Why are you hitting me?

LESLIE crosses to GUY.

LESLIE   Did Guy tell you that we bumped into each other? What was it? About eight months ago?

EVA   Looks like that to me.

GUY and LESLIE hug each other warmly while the others look on in total disbelief, miming to each other "Did you know?" "No!" "Did you?" "Why should I know?" "You see her in the city?" "How could you not know?" LESLIE turns to catch them in their gossip.

LESLIE   What?

PEGGY   Ah, Leslie, this is . . . it's just such a surprise!

(to GUY) Why didn't you tell us?

He looks at them, confused.

GUY   I didn't know.

JESSIE   You're denying it?

GUY   I'm not denying anything. I didn't know she was . . .

EVA   . . . bumped into?

GUY   What?

> *He suddenly realizes what everyone is thinking.*

Oh! Oh! No! Wait. I get it now.

> *He starts to laugh.*

JESSIE   This isn't funny.

GUY   No, it is. Really. Tell them, Leslie.

LESLIE   Tell them what?

GUY   I'm not the father.

LESLIE   You?

> *She looks at the others.*

You think Guy's? . . . Where would you come up with that?

PEGGY   He told us he *"bumped"* into you eight months ago or so out
          in LA and you never said anything to us about any of that . . .

GLORIA   . . . and then you walk in here . . .

EVA   . . . looking eight months or more pregnant!

JESSIE   What were we supposed to think?

LESLIE   That is too funny. I looked forward to surprising you but I never expected those facial reactions. Now I get it!

PEGGY   I assumed your surprise was about a new restaurant. Not motherhood! Look at you. How are you?

>*PEGGY finally hugs her, as do EVA and GLORIA, who express warm feelings about seeing her.*

LESLIE   *(while being hugged)* Actually, about nine months pregnant. And although I'm getting rather tired of hauling this around, the closer I get to my due date, the more I'm afraid I've made a huge mistake.

JESSIE   Nonsense. Motherhood agrees with you. You look absolutely joyous.

LESLIE   Mrs. Mac. It's so nice to see you. My God, it's been years.

EVA   But I saw your picture a little while ago in the paper. You didn't look pregnant.

LESLIE   You can hide a lot under those chef whites. We decided to keep it quiet until we were sure everything was all right. We got preggers before but I miscarried and it was pretty traumatic for us. We split up for a while even.

EVA   We?

LESLIE   Claude Paquette. I met him years ago at a very trendy restaurant in Montreal. His specialty was mussels and about thirty different sauces he would cook them in. We did the long-distance thing for a while and he was in the process of moving to Toronto when I miscarried. I freaked. Decided it was some kind of omen. So I ended it. I was nuts. A crazy person. He managed to get in with a hotel chain in Victoria, then LA.

(to GLORIA) Do you remember my chef friend, Joey Santos?

GLORIA   The one with the gorgeous grey hair?

(to the others) I was at Allen's late one night when Leslie introduced me to this very sexy chef from her kitchen.

EVA   Did he ask you out?

GLORIA   That would've been nice, but then his six-foot-two boyfriend came in and they went out together.

EVA   His partner works in the movie industry in LA. He uses my place for industry parties when his company is filming in the city. Joey got his green card, moved out to LA, and opened his own place. He begged me to come out to hold his hand through the restaurant-opening jitters. But when I arrived, who was sautéing mussels in his kitchen but Claude. We looked at each other and, well, that was it.

JESSIE   So love at second sight. What a wonderful story.

She looks knowingly at GUY.

Isn't that a nice story, Guy?

GUY   *(glaring at JESSIE)* Yes.

LESLIE   Guy met Claude actually. Last January when we ran into each other at . . .

GUY   . . . Joey's restaurant. That's what I was explaining just before you entered looking so . . .

LESLIE   Knocked up?

             LESLIE laughs.

             And so you all thought . . . that is just too funny.

GLORIA   When are you due?

LESLIE   Around the twentieth.

GLORIA   Will Claude be here for the birth?

LESLIE   He's flying in on Tuesday, actually. The other part of my surprise is that we've decided to settle in Montreal. He's bought into a new restaurant. I'm keeping my financial interest in Allen's but giving over the running of it to my partner for a few years. Then we'll see how everyone is coping with the changes. So this could be the last time I'll see everyone for a while. Unless you're willing to trek to Montreal to see our Jean Claude or Marie Francoise . . . whatever is in here.

EVA   I hardly get to see you as it is. Now it'll be never.

PEGGY   Nonsense. We can use this as an excuse for a girls' weekend to Quebec every year. I propose that each fall we make a pact to see Leslie. Who's in?

             GLORIA holds out her hand palm down.

GLORIA   I'm in. Especially, if it means eating mussels made by Claude.

             LESLIE laughs and puts her hand on GLORIA's.

LESLIE   No problem. How about it, Eva?

EVA   Does it also include no kids, no husbands, and lots of shopping?

LESLIE   Obviously!

          EVA slaps her hand on top of the others.

EVA   How's next weekend?

LESLIE   Let me get there first. No, first, let me get rid of this stomach. It's really starting to get in the way of my life.

PEGGY   You think it's in the way now? Wait till Jean Claude or Marie Francoise is here. You can say goodbye to your life as you know it.

LESLIE   Oh, I know all that. Actually, I'm really excited. A lot of people, insert my mother here, were concerned about me having this baby so late but, trust me, I wasn't ready at twenty-five or even thirty to mother anything. Hell, I could barely keep my house plants alive, but at almost forty . . . well, I feel . . . ready. I feel . . .

JESSIE   Tired? You look a little tired. I know it's a pyjama party but I think we should let Leslie get some sleep.

GLORIA   I agree. Leslie, take the bed in that room. I'll sleep on the cot that's in there.

EVA   Can I have the cot? That way I can gab with Les for a while. Until she falls asleep.

LESLIE   Are you sure? I'm last in. I don't mind staying here on the sofa.

GLORIA   Don't be silly. This is too soft for you. I'll sleep here.

JESSIE   I think I'll turn in as well. What about you, Margaret Anne?

PEGGY   I guess. We have to be up early tomorrow.

EVA   The party's over? It's not even midnight. I haven't dyed my hair yet.

LESLIE   Oh, don't stop because of me. I promise to be more energetic tomorrow. Can we go to Gary's Diner for breakfast?

GUY   You? The chef from Allen's wants to eat breakfast at Gary's?

LESLIE   I've been craving it ever since I left the city. Who's in for Gary's with me?

LESLIE puts her palm out to be slapped.

PEGGY   Mom and I have to organize the dresses. And Gloria and Eva were going to golf tomorrow morning.

JESSIE   *(looking at GUY)* Oh really?

JESSIE attempts to prompt GUY.

Did you book a time?

GLORIA   Yes.

EVA   No offence, Gloria, but I'd rather have breakfast with Leslie. You'll get to see her in the city before she moves. But I might not see her again until next fall.

GLORIA   That's fine, Eva. I'll cancel the tee-off time.

JESSIE crosses to GUY.

JESSIE   I'm sure Guy could help you with that, right, Guy?

GUY   Sure. No problem. Consider it cancelled.

JESSIE gives GUY a shove.

JESSIE   *(in a low voice)* Although . . .

GLORIA   Pardon?

JESSIE   Guy said, "although." Although what, Guy?

GUY   Uh . . .

JESSIE   Of course! Although . . . it would be a shame to lose your tee-off time. Maybe there's someone else who could go out with you? I'd offer but I found out tonight I'm really not very good. And, of course, Margaret Anne has the dresses, and Eva and Leslie are gonna have a good gossip session. You could join them and hear all about Eva's husband . . . again.

GLORIA grimaces.

So who's left?

They all look at GUY.

LESLIE   What about Guy?

JESSIE   What a great idea, Leslie. Of course. Why didn't I think of that? Guy would love to go out on the course with you, wouldn't you, Guy?

GUY   Uh . . .

JESSIE   See, look at this.

>*JESSIE picks up the putter.*

Gloria just bought this and she really needs to break it in.

>*They all step back as JESSIE does a rather large, awkward swing.*

>*GUY grabs the putter from her.*

GUY   I don't think I should . . .

JESSIE   Nonsense. It's okay for Guy to use your putter, isn't it, Gloria?

GLORIA   I guess.

>*JESSIE grabs it back from GUY.*

JESSIE   Maybe you could share it tomorrow. Kind of give it a double workout. Well, it's settled. *(hurriedly)* You two can get in a golf game. You two can gossip at Gary's. We two can do the dresses. And then we can all go to the church to see Kerry Larkin marry Bobby Seyfert.

PEGGY   Ma, you're quite the social planner. Maybe the girls don't wanna go.

GLORIA   Oh, I planned on it. I even brought a dress to wear. I can't wait to see your gowns on all the girls.

LESLIE   I'm going. I wanna make faces at Jimmy as he walks his daughter down the aisle. It's hard for me to believe that my old locker partner is gonna be a father-in-law.

PEGGY   Forget father-in-law. Try grandfather.

LESLIE   You're kidding? You mean? When?

JESSIE   I'd say in four months, given the last fitting.

LESLIE   Now this I definitely want to hear about. Right now, however, I just want the bathroom. I believe he or she is sitting on my bladder.

          LESLIE exits into the bathroom.

GLORIA   Come on, Eva, I saw extra sheets in the cupboard. Let's make up that cot for you.

          GLORIA exits into the bedroom.

          EVA stops at the bar and picks up a bottle of wine.

EVA   One for the road. Join me, Guy?

GUY   No. No thanks. I'm going to check on Bobby and the boys. Make sure they're behaving themselves.

EVA   Too bad. We still have so much catching up to do. If I can't sleep, maybe I'll head back down to that old hot tub. We could catch up then. Just to warn you though, I'm not putting on a wet bathing suit.

GUY   Oh.

EVA   See ya later.

            EVA exits into the bedroom.

PEGGY   Good night, Eva.

            PEGGY turns to GUY.

            Thanks for all your help today, Guy. See you at the wedding
            tomorrow.

            She starts toward her bedroom.

            Coming, Ma?

JESSIE   In a minute, dear. Just waiting for the bathroom.

            PEGGY exits and JESSIE hits GUY on the arm.

GUY   Ow! Would you quit doing that?

JESSIE   What are you doing? Making plans to sit in the hot tub with
            Eva when Gloria could've walked out here any minute.

GUY   She wasn't serious.

            A pause while he looks at EVA's door.

            Was she?

JESSIE   Did that California sun bleach your brain? Or have you
            always been this naive? Now wait here until Gloria comes
            out and then make your move.

GUY What move?

JESSIE Your move. Your strategy. Your plan. Talk to her, you idiot. Connect. Reminisce. Beg forgiveness for being eighteen and stupid. Cry. I don't know. Just communicate to her that you would like to spend more time with her.

> *LESLIE comes out of the bathroom and picks up her overnight bag.*

LESLIE Good night, Mrs. McConnell.

JESSIE Good night, dear. I hope you're able to sleep.

LESLIE It's fits and starts but I'm used to it. I'm sure the Diva will prattle on and won't even notice that I'm asleep.

> *JESSIE heads into the bathroom. LESLIE watches until the door closes then turns and gives GUY a long hug.*

How are you? How's it been going, really?

GUY Since you saw me at that AA meeting last January? Or since I've been home?

LESLIE Both.

GUY Not very anonymous when I go to my regular AA group and meet up with an old high-school friend. I never saw that coming.

LESLIE I hadn't been to one in years. But I knew the restaurant opening would be . . . stressful. Thought I needed a little help to get through that week.

GUY   So you found a meeting and you found me.

LESLIE   Looking like shit, I might add.

GUY   I did, didn't I? I came home last spring. I wanted to come see you at Allen's but it was the beginning of the season here and every week was busy. I wanted to thank you.

LESLIE   For what?

GUY   For showing up when you did. Out of nowhere. Out of a past that I thought I'd forgotten about. For listening and not judging. And for coming home and calling Jimmy. He flew out right away. Did you know that?

LESLIE   I didn't know that. I just knew Jimmy. You don't share a locker for all those years with someone and not know him. You seemed so alone out there. I just thought you needed some support. You needed a brother.

GUY   He brought me home. Or, at least, he gave me a reason to come home. The lodge keeps me busy. And I've been thinking of putting out the shingle again. Jim said I could turn one of the front suites into an office. We've been trying to come up with a slogan: "Come for a weekend retreat and plan your will at the same time."

> LESLIE *laughs.*

I know. Too long.

LESLIE   How about "Wellness and Wills"?

GUY   Now that I like. I wonder if Jimmy'd go for a name change to this place?

LESLIE   And your wife? How did that turn out?

GUY   Badly at first. But since I've been home things have gotten
          better. Sometimes long-distance geography can solve a lot of
          problems. She's with a decent guy, now. He was an accoun-
          tant at the firm. Maybe a little boring, but after living with
          me I can understand why she's choosing him. Actually, I
          like him. And he's great with Justine. Who I will get to see
          next month. Her mother has agreed to visit her family in
          Chicago for American Thanksgiving. I'm flying there for
          the weekend. I get to take them out to lunch, maybe the
          aquarium, a movie. Whatever Justine wants.

LESLIE   So your sad story has a good ending?

GUY   I like to think of it as a new beginning. Each day. One day . . .

          She finishes with him.

LESLIE   . . . at a time.

          They smile.

GUY   I go to the meetings here. You wouldn't believe who I see.
          But then again, you probably would.

LESLIE   *(hugging him)* I'm glad for you, Guy. That little girl needs to
          know her dad. Trust me. This comes from someone whose
          father walked out on his family when she was four. And look
          what happened to me.

GUY   Bad argument, Les. You're the richest and most successful
          of anyone in our class.

LESLIE   With a lot of crap that I hid from a lot of people for a long
          time. Look at you, a California lawyer.

GUY   With a lot of crap that I hid from a lot of people . . .

LESLIE   *(together)* . . . for a long time.

          Beat.

          But I think we're gonna make it, Guy. I'm hopeful. Are you?

GUY   I want to be.

          *JESSIE comes out of the bathroom and makes her way to her
          purse, which she puts in the refrigerator during the following.
          The others watch her with interest.*

JESSIE   Oh, still here? Well, good night again, Leslie. Guy, why
          don't you stay until Gloria comes out? Make sure she's clear
          about the golf game tomorrow. It would be a shame to have
          the wrong tee-off time.

          *JESSIE looks meaningfully at him and then exits into the
          bedroom.*

          LELIE gathers her things.

LESLIE   I think Mrs. Mac has the right idea for you.

GUY   Playing golf?

LESLIE   Trying to match you up with Gloria Atherly.

GUY   It's that obvious?

LESLIE   Gloria's great. She would be good for you. She stuck by me when I was pretty crazy. She understands pain and loss. She was pretty stoic when Charlie was killed but I could see it in her eyes. She was devastated. But if you're thinking of asking Gloria out, be honest with her, Guy.

GUY   Her husband was killed by a drunk driver and you want me to tell her who I am? Hey, Gloria, how about a movie next Saturday night and, by the way, I could've been the guy who drove the car that killed your husband. Just thought you should know. How're my chances of scoring that date?

LESLIE   Be honest. Not brutal. Why don't you begin by telling her why you came home? And while you're at it, you could apologize for not showing up for the prom.

GUY   Not that again. We both know I found other things to indulge in that night.

LESLIE   I know. I was there, and although it's foggy, I do recollect some serious hash that had been scored from the city.

GUY   You see, even then, you and me on the same path of self-destruction.

LESLIE   I do remember making it out here later that night and all the girls were sitting in this room, looking at that door, knowing Gloria was in there crying her heart out.

GUY   I did come out to apologize.

LESLIE   It was four in the morning and you were wasted. Yelling her name from the dock below. *Glooorrrryyyyy!* And then laughing hysterically.

GUY   I was trying to be Marlon Brando.

LESLIE   We weren't impressed. Poor Gloria standing in the middle of the room with the girlfriends all around her. It looked like a scene out of *Wagon Train* except she was encircled by feminine rage. You didn't stand a chance, my boy. It was a shitty way to end your friendship, let alone your teenage romance. Apologize for that. Trust me, even after all this time, she, at least, needs to hear that from you.

         GLORIA enters from the bedroom.

GLORIA   Did you call me, Leslie?

LESLIE   Uh . . . no. Well . . . I'm exhausted. Good night, Guy.

         LESLIE kisses him.

         Thanks for the talk. You really are a sweet man.

         She exits into the bedroom.

         GLORIA watches her go.

GLORIA   That's the second woman today who's called you a sweet man.

GUY   Me?

GLORIA   Yeah, hard to believe, isn't it?

GUY   Oh, I don't know. Is it?

         GLORIA stares at GUY. A long pause.

         So . . .

GUY sees her putter and picks it up.

I had my eye on this one too.

GLORIA Really? I didn't know you played that much.

GUY Oh, I don't. But just thought this looked like a good one.

He takes a few practice swings.

GLORIA You're breaking your wrist.

GUY What?

GLORIA And you're bringing your head up too early. You're probably one of those golfers, more interested in where the ball is going rather than making the solid contact.

GUY You can tell that. That I'm one of *those* kinds of golfers?

GLORIA Yes.

GUY So how do I fix it?

GLORIA Concentrate on your spine. Keep your back long.

She places her hand on his back while he follows through, and just as the club is above the imaginary ball she stops him.

Stop there. Do you feel my hand along the length of your back?

She gently rubs up and down his back.

A pause as he enjoys this.

GUY   Oh, yeah.

Suddenly realizing her position with him, GLORIA takes away the putter.

GLORIA   You really don't play much, do you? Why'd you agree to go out tomorrow?

GUY   I didn't want you to lose your tee-off time and I thought you'd give me some pointers. You were always better at sports. Now that I'm home, I should take more interest in the golf course.

GLORIA   I didn't know there would be a lot of legal issues around the golf course.

GUY   Oh sure.

GLORIA   Like what?

GUY   Uh . . . accident insurance . . . getting smacked by a ball, run over by a cart . . . uh . . . environmental issues . . . smacking a goose with a ball. Those geese are vicious in court, you know. They've got litigation down to a fine art. The way they come at you . . .

He forms a vee with his arms. GLORIA is not impressed.

GLORIA   Perhaps you'd better stay clear of the course then in case you run into some former adversaries. It'd be bad enough losing to me let alone being chased down the fairway by some angry gander.

GUY   Losing to you?

GLORIA   You admitted you don't play and that I was always better at
         sports, so yes, I would beat you. And you can even use the
         ladies' tees.

GUY   Care to make a small wager on that statement?

GLORIA   No. I'll make a big one, though. Unless you're not financially
         able at this time to . . .

GUY   How much?

GLORIA   A hundred bucks and the winner names the charity.

GUY   Fine. Bring your chequebook.

GLORIA   You can start filling yours out now. To the Society for the
         Preservation of Canadian Geese.

GUY   You're making that up.

GLORIA   Wanna bet another hundred?

         Beat.

GUY   No.

GLORIA   Fine.

GUY   So . . . this'll be fun. Actually, I was hoping to spend some
         time with you, Glory. Just to talk. Catch up. You know.

GLORIA   Talk? About what?

GUY   Lots of things. Life. Yours. Mine. What's happened over
         the years.

GLORIA   There's not much to say, is there. I left Woodsville, graduated with an economics degree, married Charlie McAllister. He died five years ago in a car accident. I work for a big bank. Your turn.

GUY   That's it? I don't think I could summarize my . . .

GLORIA   Sure you could. You moved to BC. Graduated with a law degree. Moved to Los Angeles. Eventually married. And apparently you are now divorced and living back here with your brother and his wife, running the Larkin Lodge. See? We already know about each other's lives. So, if there's not another topic of conversation, I could really use some sleep if we're golfing in the morning.

GUY   Wait a minute. Don't you think you left out some of the details in your brief chronicle of our life and times?

GLORIA   The details aren't important.

GUY   Not important?

GLORIA   Look, Guy, I'm sorry that your marriage didn't work out, but the reason or reasons are not my concern. I'm sorry that you chased your dream to sunny California and apparently your career didn't work out and you're back here now. I'm sorry that at middle age you're living with your brother's family. I'm sorry . . .

GUY   You feel sorry for me? That's it? You judge my life on generalities, without knowing the details, and decide that ultimately I should be pitied? And I'm not middle-aged.

GLORIA   We're all turning forty this year. Look, that's not how I meant it.

GUY   Well, I feel sorry for you.

GLORIA   Why? Because I'm widowed? Oh please, your condolences would've been better appreciated five years ago when the accident happened. But I don't recall hearing from you then. But better late than never, right?

GUY   I feel sorry that you've become so cold.

> *She glares at him.*

Yes, I feel sorry for you that Charlie died. That he was taken so horribly and suddenly. That you were left alone. And, yes, I feel shallow for not writing to you. For not extending sincerest sympathies. For not signing a card saying my thoughts are with you in your time of sorrow. But, Glory, you had to know they were. You had to know that.

> *Pause.*

I felt paralyzed when I heard about Charlie. I couldn't write to you because I was involved in a criminal case dealing with the same issue at the time.

GLORIA   You were defending a drunk driver?

GUY   No. I was the drunk driver.

GLORIA   You killed someone?

GUY   No. I destroyed a car and sent someone to a hospital. Me.

GLORIA   What happened?

GUY   That's a detailed answer. Are you sure you want details?

GLORIA   Not if you don't want to tell me. It's really none of my business.

GUY   But it is your business, Glory. You need to know why I never contacted you when Charlie died. You need to know what happened to me in California. I need for you to know it. All of it. Just like I need to know what happened to you. How did you get through all that? God, I need to know why you married Charlie McAllister in the first place. He was such a geek in high school.

GLORIA   *(laughing)* That's right, you never saw Charlie after graduation, did you? Charlie McAllister was one of those guys who just exploded into himself after high school. Somewhere along the way he became confident, successful. He even grew taller. Six two. We met at a banking conference and he admitted that he'd had a crush on me forever. Pursued me like no one ever had before in my life, and one day I suddenly realized that Charlie was the kindest person I'd ever known. Not just to me but to everyone he met. I fell in love with him for being like that.

> *Beat.*

More than anything, I miss his kindness yet.

GUY   So . . . Charlie McAllister grew to be six two. You see, that's a detail that I never knew. Tell you what we need to do.

> *He goes to the table and finds some paper and two pens.*

We're going to write out five questions that we want the other person to answer about their life. When we have the questions ready, we'll take turns asking them. And we have to be honest with each other. No glossing over details. The details are what we need.

GLORIA   Guy, it's late and . . .

GUY   Five questions, that's all. Here.

He hands her paper and a pen.

Beat.

GLORIA   Five questions?

GUY   Five. So think carefully about what you want to ask. I promise I'll let you turn in when we're done.

They sit on opposite sides of the couch, backs to each other. GUY looks skyward trying to phrase his first question. He writes something and looks at it proudly. GLORIA writes furiously and finishes her five questions in seconds.

GLORIA   Done.

GUY   What? You've got five questions already? Let's see.

GLORIA   Uh uh. Not fair. You can't see them. You're not going to prepare answers ahead of time. How many have you got?

GUY   One.

GLORIA   That's all. After all these years you could only come up with one question to ask me?

GUY   Give me a second. I'll think of some more.

He looks at his sheet, struggling to think of something to write. She stares at him.

It's a little difficult to concentrate when you're glaring at me like that.

He returns to his sheet and begins to write, then suddenly changes his mind and vehemently crosses out what he has written.

GLORIA   Oh, you're impossible. This isn't going to work. Why don't you take your paper with you, think up four more questions, and I'll answer them while we're golfing tomorrow.

GUY   No. Tell you what. Why don't we start with your questions and when one comes to me while I'm answering yours, then I'll write it down. I promise not to ask you the same questions you ask me. Okay?

GLORIA   *(hesitant)* All right. I guess.

GUY   Great.

GUY makes himself comfortable.

So you go first. Shoot. What's your first question?

Without looking at her sheet.

GLORIA   Why did you abandon me at our prom?

Pause.

GUY   Right. Okay. Somehow I knew that was going to be one of the questions on your list. Just didn't expect it to be the first. All right. Let's see. Where should I start?

GLORIA   No glossing. Details. You said I could expect details.

GUY   You're right. This one may take some time though, because
          before I can explain the details of that particular night, I
          need to go into a lot of family history and stuff.

GLORIA   Stuff?

GUY   Nature versus nurture kind of stuff. Or in my case the influ-
          ences of both.

GLORIA   Should I go on to my second question? I'm getting the feeling
          this first one is going to be glossed over.

GUY   No. No. I just need to set the time. The historical context if
          you would.

GLORIA   Do you waste this much time in the courtroom?

GUY   My dad. Great guy. When he was sober. The problem was
          he wasn't sober a lot of the time. Most nights he'd come
          home, disappear to the basement, and we never knew what
          was going to emerge on the other side.

GLORIA   And what? He got drunk the night of the prom?

GUY   When you grow up in an environment like that, like I did,
          you start to think of it as normal. Of drinking a twelve-pack
          a night as okay. Dad does it so I should be able to do it too. I
          think genetically I was linked to my dad in that way. Except
          for me, it wasn't so much the booze as the drugs. I was using
          in high school. You knew that.

GLORIA   Well, we all used a little in high school.

GUY   No, you all used on an occasional weekend if someone scored something. I used every day. Whether it was a joint or vodka, I used it daily. On the night of the prom I had a chance to score some really good hash. And it was higher on my list of priorities than seeing you in a pretty dress. I got carried away. By the time I realized what was happening I came out here to apologize but it was way too late. And the next day I was still too stoned, too embarrassed, too much of a coward to redeem myself. So I never ever did. Until now. I'm . . . I'm sorry for that night, Gloria. And I'm saying this not because it's part of the program . . . making amends and all . . . but because I really am. So sorry. It was a lousy thing to do to you.

         A beat as she looks at him.

GLORIA   Yeah. It was.

         Pause.

         I have a question about this game.

GUY   What?

GLORIA   What if the answer to the question raises more questions? Am I allowed to ask subquestions?

GUY   That's the beauty of this game, Glory. You can ask me as many questions as you want.

GLORIA   All right. Then explain this to me. Why the sudden move to BC?

GUY   My mother. She realized what was happening and sent me out to her brother. Uncle Greg. Ex-military. She knew he'd straighten me out. And he did. He put me to work, hard labour at his mill. After a year I suggested university. He agreed. Watched me like a hawk. I got into a great firm in Vancouver with a subsidiary in LA and by the time I was writing the California bar exam, I'd been clean and sober for years. But LA is not the greatest place to be when you're lonely and stressed and have . . . issues.

GLORIA   You started using again. Were you married then?

GUY   Is my marriage one of your five questions?

GLORIA   Could be. Tell me about your wife.

GUY   I'm afraid to. You'll probably hate me after you hear what I put her through.

GLORIA   How do you know I don't already hate you?

GUY   Fair enough. My wife was a secretary at the firm. A really beautiful, sweet girl. All the guys were interested in her but, for some reason, she took to me. Maybe it was my Canadian charm, eh?

          GLORIA gives him a look.

          Or not. I was already starting to behave a little carelessly and, for some reason, she found that attractive.

GLORIA   Maybe she wanted to fix you. Save you. Some women are like that. Think they can change the men in their lives.

GUY   Sadly for her that didn't happen. We married too quickly. Had a child too quickly. All of which added to the stress in my life. But luckily for her, she was smart enough to know when to walk away. And so she did. Which gave me even more reasons to continue behaving badly, until I woke up in a hospital after a particularly spectacular car crash on a coastal California highway.

GLORIA   And you were charged with drunk driving?

GUY   Reckless driving but not impaired. Because I had access to a high-level legal team, the case managed to go away. And then they suggested I do the same thing.

GLORIA   They fired you?

GUY   Suggested I seek employment elsewhere. Which I knew wouldn't happen unless I shaped up. So I took some time to get help. That's where Leslie comes in. When she saw me in LA, she took one look at me and immediately called Jim.

GLORIA   Who brought you home.

GUY   Home. Yes.

           Beat.

           So do all those details answer your first question?

GLORIA   I guess. Do you want to ask your one question now?

GUY   No. I need more time. Why don't you keep going?

           She stares at GUY *then refers to her list.*

GLORIA   Okay, here's the next thing I'd like to ask about. Your daughter.

GUY smiles and the lights begin to fade as GUY begins.

GUY   Justine. Justine is awesome. She's seven now, and as beautiful as her mom. I talk to her on the phone quite a bit and she's learning about email and Skyping. I'm planning on seeing her next month when . . .

Blackout.

SCENE 2

Lights come up to find GUY and GLORIA asleep on the sofa. GLORIA is snuggled sideways into the crook of his arm with her hand on his chest. LESLIE enters from the bedroom and begins to cross to the bathroom. She sees them and smiles. She drapes a blanket over them and continues to the bathroom. GUY stretches his free arm over his head and opens his eyes. He looks around, remembering where he is, and sees GLORIA asleep on him. He's not sure what to do. He moves slightly to see if he can move his arm away, and as he does so GLORIA opens her eyes. There is a long, awkward moment as they look at each other.

GLORIA   I got cold.

She moves away from him.

GUY   That's all right.

Pause.

Sorry, I don't remember drifting off.

GLORIA   I think it was during question five. Subquestion nine.

GUY   Oh, right. Did I finish that answer?

GLORIA   I think so.

An awkward pause as they look at each other.

Well . . . I wonder what it's like out?

She scrambles off of the sofa and goes to the window, opening the drapes.

Sunshine for the wedding. Are you still up for the golf? We don't have to if . . .

GUY   Wouldn't miss it.

He heads for the door.

I'll just get changed and meet you at the pro shop in thirty minutes? Do you want to grab some breakfast first?

He has opened the door as JESSIE appears fully dressed in casual clothes from her bedroom. She looks at them approvingly.

JESSIE   Good morning. Good morning. How'd you sleep, Gloria?

GLORIA   Fine.

JESSIE   Good.

(to GUY) You're here bright and early. Aren't you a little over-dressed for a golf game?

GUY   Uh . . . *(looking at GLORIA)* . . . yeah. Well, you see, what happened was . . .

> *There is a loud scream from the bathroom.*

JESSIE   My God. Who's that?

> *JESSIE crosses over to the bathroom door and knocks on it. The others follow.*

Hello?

LESLIE   It's me, Mrs. McConnell. Could you come in here, please. Quick!

> *She turns to GLORIA.*

JESSIE   She wants me to go in.

> *GLORIA motions for her to do so. JESSIE enters the bathroom. GLORIA and GUY look at each other. PEGGY enters from the bedroom wearing track pants and putting on a sweatshirt as EVA follows in her pyjamas.*

PEGGY   What the hell was that noise?

GUY   It's Leslie.

GLORIA   She's in the bathroom.

GUY   With your mother.

PEGGY crosses to the door.

PEGGY   Ma, are you okay? Is everything all right?

PEGGY comes out from the bathroom.

JESSIE   We have a bit of an emergency. Leslie's water just broke. I think we need to get her to the hospital right away.

EVA   Is she okay?

JESSIE   A little startled but she'll be fine. She's just going to have her baby now instead of in two weeks. Guy, I think it's best if you do the driving. Go and get Jimmy's van and warm it up. Meet us at the bottom of the stairs.

GUY runs for the door.

GUY   I'm on it, Mrs. Mac. Anything else?

JESSIE   Ask Pat for some extra towels. Just in case.

He looks at her in horror.

GUY   Oh my God!

He races out the door.

JESSIE   *(to GLORIA and EVA)* Gather up Leslie's bag and things. Find her coat.

They run to the bedroom.

(to PEGGY) Leslie wants me to come with her to the hospital until her mother arrives. She can call her on the way.

PEGGY   I'll follow in my car. Let me get my purse.

PEGGY heads to the bedroom. GLORIA returns with LESLIE's coat.

JESSIE   You have to stay here. The dresses for Kerry's wedding.

PEGGY   They're fine. I can take them down to Pat right now. She can find someone to help her.

GLORIA   You go.

EVA enters with the bag.

Eva and I can help Kerry and the girls.

PEGGY races to the bedroom for her purse. GLORIA grabs a paper from the sofa and writes. The bathroom door opens and LESLIE enters. JESSIE attempts to put the coat on LESLIE.

LESLIE   But I'm not properly dressed. I only have my slippers on, for God's sakes.

EVA   Your shoes are in your bag.

LESLIE heads over to EVA. JESSIE follows, trying to guide LESLIE to the door.

JESSIE   I can put your shoes on you in the van. Gloria, take Leslie's bag and see if Guy's ready.

GLORIA hands the paper to JESSIE.

GLORIA   Keep in contact. Here's my cell number. Call me.

GLORIA heads out the door. PEGGY returns from the bedroom.

PEGGY   How're you doing, Les?

LESLIE   I'm not ready to have the baby today. I have to be back at the
          restaurant at six.

JESSIE   You'll have to forego that, dear. I think you're going to be
          busy elsewhere.

LESLIE   But . . .

JESSIE   That's it. Keep walking. Margaret Anne's going to go ahead of
          us and let them know that you're arriving. She'll get a wheel-
          chair ready. While we're driving to the hospital, you can give
          me the names of everyone who needs to be called and she can
          take care of all that when we get there, right, Margaret Anne?

PEGGY   Yeah. Don't worry, Les, you're in good hands. Ma'll take
          good care of you.

          *PEGGY heads out the door. JESSIE guides LESLIE toward the
          door and their conversation continues as we see them go past
          the window.*

LESLIE   But I don't want to have the baby today. Claude's coming
          on Tuesday. Can't I have it on Tuesday? I want to go to the
          wedding.

JESSIE   Oh, I'm sure we'll hear all about it. Gloria will take lots of pic-
          tures. Now all we have to do is get down these damned stairs.

          EVA is left alone, standing in the doorway.

          There is total silence.

EVA   Wow!

EVA looks around and decides to take off her wig when suddenly a cellphone rings an offbeat tune. She finds her purse in the kitchen and pulls it out. She does not see JESSIE, who has returned and is shocked to see EVA. She stands in the doorway.

Hi! How's it going, Stevie, my sweetie? . . . What? When? . . . How's he doin'? . . . Okay, I'll head home right after the ceremony . . . No, it's fine, sweetie . . . Last night? It was fun. I missed you though . . . The others—

She turns and suddenly sees JESSIE.

Uh . . . there's been a bit of an emergency here as well. I'll call you back . . . Me too.

She hangs up.

JESSIE I forgot my purse.

EVA My five-year-old has the flu.

JESSIE Oh. I'm sorry to hear that. But your husband's there. Steve, the one you were calling sweetie?

EVA Uh . . . yeah.

JESSIE The one you've been complaining about? He's actually a sweetie?

EVA Look, Mrs. Mac. I have a love-hate relationship with these reunions. Every time I meet up with my old high-school friends I find they want me to be Eva the Diva because that's who I was.

JESSIE I remember her, Eva, only too well.

Beat.

EVA   That day. You found me . . . in the second floor washroom . . . with . . . And you never reported it. Why?

JESSIE   It was coming up to final exams. You would've been suspended. Seemed like a high price to pay for being . . .

EVA   Stupid.

JESSIE   For being young.

EVA   I was terrified of you. I was afraid you'd tell . . .

JESSIE   Your parents?

EVA   No. I was afraid you'd tell Peggy. But you never did.

JESSIE   No. I never did.

EVA   Thank you for that.

         EVA holds up her wig

I'm not really this girl anymore. After that first disastrous marriage, I met Steve. Quiet, dependable, responsible Steve, and I became, well, just Eva. Calm, happy wife and mother. But there's a part of me—

         She holds up her wig.

—that loves being this girl again. Even if it's just for a night. She's loud and funny and outrageous . . . but she's also . . .

JESSIE   ... Exhausting? Eva, dear, I suspect that the girls may be a little tired of the Diva as well.

EVA   But I thought she kept us all young.

JESSIE   Young? You're all turning forty. She's hard to keep up with. Maybe it's time you started to let them know the real Eva. I think they'd like her.

She takes EVA's hand.

She seems pretty special. Worrying about her little boy.

EVA   Not too boring?

JESSIE   Not at all. I hope she's the one I see from now on.

EVA hugs JESSIE. PEGGY runs past the window and appears in the doorway, somewhat surprised at seeing these two together.

PEGGY   Ma! What's taking so long? Did you lose your purse?

JESSIE   No, it's right here.

JESSIE opens the refrigerator and removes her purse.

PEGGY   Ma, why do you keep putting your purse in the refrigerator?

JESSIE   Because I read somewhere that it's the safest place to put it when you're travelling or when you have strange workmen in the house.

PEGGY   And the day Kerry was there for her fitting? Wasn't the furnace guy in the basement?

JESSIE   Yes, for the annual checkup. Why are you asking?

PEGGY   Uh . . . no reason.

EVA   Smart move, Mrs. Mac. I'm gonna remember that from now on!

A car horn sounds loudly.

PEGGY   Oh my gosh, we'd better go before Leslie has this baby in the van. Try to keep her calm on the drive, Ma.

JESSIE   No problem. I'll sing all the Broadway tunes I know.

JESSIE hurries out humming one of them. PEGGY stares at EVA.

PEGGY   So . . . not really a diva after all?

EVA   No. Just . . . me. Just Eva.

PEGGY   And just Eva is the one who hugs my mother?

EVA   *(laughing)* Yeah. How about that? I'm glad you brought her, Peg. If anyone was gonna get rid of the Diva, it would be her. She's . . . she's a very smart person. You're lucky to still have her in your life.

PEGGY   Yes, I am. Tell Jimmy we'll be back soon. We won't miss the wedding.

EVA   Gotcha.

PEGGY exits and EVA picks up her phone and dials.

Hi, sweetie! Sorry I had to hang up earlier but we're having a baby here . . . Leslie . . . Yes, she just left for the hospital . . . She'll be fine. Peggy's mom's with her so she's definitely in good hands . . . I could come home now and skip the wedding . . . Really? Are you sure? . . . Oh, Steve, you're too good!

EVA looks at her wig.

Tell you what, for being a super dad and a super husband I'll have a special reward for you tonight . . . You'll find out . . . Let's just say it's a final performance . . . Of what? . . .

In her best Southern accent.

I'm calling it the Kindness of a Red-Headed Stranger . . .

She laughs.

Me too! See you later, darlin'.

She hangs up and starts toward her room, tossing her wig in the air.

Nice to know she's still there . . . when I need her!

She exits to the bedroom.

Blackout.

SCENE 3

Lights up on the cabin later that afternoon. The sound of a hair dryer comes from the bathroom door. JESSIE, dressed for the wedding, comes out of her bedroom. A muffled ringing cellphone is heard. She follows it to GLORIA's purse. She holds up the purse and walks toward the bathroom door.

JESSIE   Gloria!

(louder) Gloria!

The hair dryer stops. GLORIA appears in the bathroom door. She is also ready for the wedding, except for three rather large curlers on the top of her head.

GLORIA   Did you call me?

JESSIE   Your purse is ringing. Maybe it's the hospital.

GLORIA comes into the room and struggles with the purse, trying to find the phone.

GLORIA   Oh, God . . . Hello? Hello? . . . No, Eva, no news . . . Yes, Eva, as soon as I hear . . . Are the girls dressed? . . . Soon. I'm still getting ready. Bye. God, this is the third time she's called in the last half hour. When is this baby going to come?

PEGGY comes out of her bedroom dressed for the wedding.

PEGGY   Is there a baby?

JESSIE   No. First baby could take a few hours yet.

PEGGY   What if the baby comes during the wedding? How rude
             would it be to keep our cellphones on in church?

GLORIA   Maybe if we sit right at the back no one'll notice. I'll keep
             mine on vibrate. If I jump up suddenly, you'll know why.

PEGGY   *(suddenly realizing)* I left mine in the car. I'll take it into the
             church, too. We should get going, Ma. I promised Kerry
             I'd meet her and the girls at the back of the church for any
             last-minute adjustments. You head down to the car. I'll get
             my coat.

             PEGGY heads into her bedroom.

JESSIE   Okay, dear. Oh, Gloria, before I forget, I think this is yours.

             *JESSIE pulls out a piece of paper from her pocket and gives
             it to GLORIA.*

GLORIA   It's just my cell number. This is the paper I gave to you.

JESSIE   It's what's on the back. I didn't know if it was important to
             you or not.

             *GLORIA turns the paper over and reads what's written on
             it out loud.*

GLORIA   "Will you be my date for the wedding?"

             Beat.

             Oh.

JESSIE   One question. At the top of the page like that. Just seemed
             peculiar. Did you write it?

GLORIA   No.

JESSIE   Oh.

      JESSIE looks at her.

      Suddenly GUY, *formally dressed for the wedding, rushes past the window and through the door.*

GUY   It's a boy! It's *(French)* Guy Claude. But it could be *(English)* "Guy" Claude.

JESSIE   A boy?

      PEGGY runs from the bedroom while putting on her jacket.

PEGGY   Leslie had it?

GUY   Yeah. She tried to call you and then Gloria, but your line was busy.

GLORIA   Eva! Ahhh! How is she? Did you talk to her?

GUY   Yeah. She sounded great. She put the phone to the baby so I could hear little Guy Claude breathing.

PEGGY   What are you talking about? I thought they had decided on Jean.

GUY   Leslie was so relieved that I got her to the hospital, she said she'd name the baby after me. Only in French. It's not official yet. She has to argue with Claude. But knowing Leslie, she'll win.

JESSIE   That's wonderful, Guy. You're sort of a godfather in name.

GUY   Yeah. How about that?

PEGGY   Can we phone her? Do you know what room she's in?

GUY   She said she'd call you later. After the wedding.

PEGGY   Thanks for running up with the news, Guy. Wow! Don't you look handsome? Are you on your way?

GUY   Yeah. In a couple of minutes.

PEGGY   Well, let's go, Ma. The girls'll be waiting. Don't forget your purse. Is it in the fridge?

> *JESSIE heads into the bedroom.*

JESSIE   No, in here. And I'll get my jacket. I'm right behind you.

PEGGY   *(to GLORIA)* Maybe we can drive over to see Leslie after the ceremony?

> *GLORIA looks at GUY.*

GLORIA   Uh . . . let's talk about it at the church, okay?

> *PEGGY exits the cabin.*

> *There is an awkward moment as GUY and GLORIA face each other.*

GUY   So . . . Leslie . . . Wow.

GLORIA   Yeah . . . Wow.

GUY   So you're gonna go see her?

GLORIA   She might be too tired. Might be better if we go tomorrow.

GUY   Yeah? Because I was wondering . . . that is, if you think you should wait until tomorrow to go . . . I thought that maybe . . .

> *JESSIE enters from the bedroom as she's putting on her jacket.*

JESSIE   Well, I'm off. I suppose you'll be on your way soon. Gloria, you might want to . . .

> *JESSIE motions to GLORIA's hair rollers, but GLORIA does not take her eyes off GUY.*

> *GUY stares at GLORIA.*

GUY   Goodbye, Mrs. Mac.

> *JESSIE suddenly realizes she is in the middle of something important.*

JESSIE   Oh, I see. Yes. Well. Goodbye, you two. See you at the church.

> *She hurries out the door and crosses in front of the window when she suddenly sees that she doesn't have her purse. She turns to go back in the room but realizes that she might be interrupting the two inside. She looks helplessly between the parking lot and the door and then turns her attention to GLORIA and GUY.*

GUY   Where were we?

GLORIA   Yes.

GUY   What?

GLORIA   The answer to your question. Yes.

GUY   But I didn't even ask you a question.

GLORIA   Yes, you did. Last night. We just never got to it. Until now.

           She holds up the paper.

           After all these years, this was the only question you could
           come up with?

GUY   It was the only one that mattered. All the other ones would've
           been about the past. This one was about tomorrow. Or, I
           guess now, today. And you're saying yes?

GLORIA   Yes.

GUY   I really want to kiss you at this moment. But I can't.

GLORIA   Why not?

GUY   Because Mrs. Mac is staring at us through the window.

           A car horn sounds impatiently. JESSIE *looks toward it and
           suddenly turns toward the door. She enters.*

JESSIE   I'm not here. I'm not here. Silly me. I forgot my purse. I'll
           just be a second.

           JESSIE *goes to her room, but not before giving* GUY *a
           thumbs up.*

GUY   I'm having a déjà vu moment. It feels like that time I saw you on the other side of Main Street. And I wanted to cross over to talk to you. But then that transport came along and blocked you from me, and when it moved forward you were gone. I feel like if I don't cross over to that side of the room in the next two seconds . . .

> *GLORIA is oblivious to JESSIE, who is tiptoeing out of the room whispering to GUY, "I'm not here."*

GLORIA   But we're not on Main Street. And there isn't any truck.

GUY   Trust me. There is.

> *JESSIE backs out the door, motioning for GUY to make his move. She closes the door and crosses in front of the window.*

GLORIA   Is it gone?

> *A beat as he expects JESSIE to return to the window.*

GUY   I think so.

GLORIA   Well, then?

> *She gives him her awkward nod.*
>
> *He smiles and nods in return. Then he strides over to her, takes her face in his hands, and gives her a long, lingering kiss.*
>
> *JESSIE reappears at the window, obviously pleased. She turns to go, then suddenly stops and walks to the cabin door. She opens it, steps in, and begins humming before breaking out into song:*

JESSIE   *(singing)* " . . . the second time around.
              And Gloria, dear, you've got some rollers in your hair . . . "

          GLORIA and GUY laugh and hug each other as the lights fade to black.

          Blackout.

          End of play.

ACKNOWLEDGEMENTS

I would like to thank Ron Cameron-Lewis for dramaturgical support at the Aurora Cultural Centre's 2008 Writers' Springboard; Jane Carnwath and Brandon Moore, who organized the readings and casts who offered much for me to think about in our discussions; and, especially, Annette Procunier for her dramaturgy after the readings at the 2013 Writers' Springboard. I would also like to thank the production support received from the Alumnae Theatre's 2012 New Ideas Festival, specifically Brenda Darling, Pat McCarthy, and Carolyn Zapf for their work in producing the festival. Thank you to FireWorks 2013 and all those involved in this first full production of the play; to the many involved with the readings produced at the Aurora Cultural Centre's 2013 Writers' Springboard; to the cast and crew of the production by the Blackhorse Village Players in 2016, especially Denise Kennedy, my stage manager, who recorded ALL of my revisions; and to Marnie Jutzi and Alison Jutzi at the Guelph Little Theatre, 2018. And to all those, too numerous to mention, who helped with the various readings over the years.

Joan Burrows is a member of the Playwrights Guild of Canada and has won several ACT-CO and Theatre Ontario awards for her work as a stage manager, director, and playwright. She has also been a long-time volunteer with TAPA (Toronto Alliance for the Performing Arts). Her other plays include *Staff Room*, *The Photograph*, *Willow Quartet*, and *Four Hours*. She is currently working on a musical adaptation of *Willow Quartet* with Ron Cameron-Lewis and Jason Saunders at Sheridan College and completing her sixth play, *Persons of Interest*, a comedy about the American Internal Revenue Service.

First edition: March 2018
Printed and bound in Canada by Rapido Books, Montreal

Jacket art by Megan Stulberg

 **PLAYWRIGHTS**
CANADA PRESS
202-269 Richmond St. W.
Toronto, ON
M5V 1X1

416.703.0013
info@playwrightscanada.com
www.playwrightscanada.com
@playcanpress